Buying a Computer That's Right for You

Shelley O'Hara

*A Division of Macmillan Computer Publishing
with a Prentice Hall Macmillan Company*

201 West 103rd Street, Indianapolis, Indiana 46290 USA

For Alana, Stephanie, and Michael

©1994 by Que Corporation

All rights reserved. No part of this book shall be reproduced, stored in a retrieval system, or transmitted by any means, electronic, mechanical, photocopying, recording, or otherwise, without written permission from the publisher. No patent liability is assumed with respect to the use of the information contained herein. Although every precaution has been taken in the preparation of this book, the publisher and author assume no responsibility for errors or omissions. Neither is any liability assumed for damages resulting from the use of the information contained herein. For information, address Que Corporation, 201 West 103rd Street, Indianapolis, Indiana 46290.

International Standard Book Number: 1-56761-500-7

Library of Congress Catalog Card Number: 94-71432

97   8 7 6

Interpretation of the printing code: the rightmost number of the second series of numbers is the number of the book's printing. For example, a printing code of 94-1 shows that the first printing of the book occurred in 1994.

Printed in the United States of America

All terms mentioned in this book that are known to be trademarks have been appropriately capitalized. Que Books cannot attest to the accuracy of this information. Use of a term in this book should not be regarded as affecting the validity of any trademark or service mark.

Screen reproductions in this book were created by means of the program Collage Plus from Inner Media, Inc., Hollis, NH.

Publisher: Marie Butler-Knight
Managing Editor: Elizabeth Keaffaber
Product Development Manager: Faithe Wempen
Acquisitions Manager: Barry Pruett
Development Editor: Kelly Oliver
Manuscript Editor: San Dee Phillips
Book Designer: Barbara Webster
Index: Rebecca Mayfield
Production: Gary Adair, Dan Caparo, Brad Chinn, Kim Cofer, Lisa Daugherty, Jennifer Eberhardt, Beth Rago, Bobbi Saterfield, Kris Simmons, Carol Stamile, Robert Wolf

Special thanks to Michael Hanks for ensuring the technical accuracy of this book.

Contents

Introduction, vii

1 Do I Need a Computer?, 1
What Is a Computer?, 1
What a Computer Can Do, 2
Benefits to Using a Computer, 3
Reasons You Want to Buy a Computer, 6
Reasons Not to Buy a Computer, 7
Summary Checklist, 7

2 What Do I Want the Computer to Do?, 9
Software You Need, 9
Types of Application Software, 10
Deciding What You Want to Do, 18
Summary Checklist, 19

3 How to Select Software, 21
Picking a Software Package, 21
Some Popular Packages, 23
Decoding the Software Requirements, 26
Summary Checklist, 28

4 Understanding Computers, 30
What Is Hardware?, 30
How a Computer Works, 31
A Personal Computer Timeline, 32

5 Types of Computers, 34
Summarizing the Differences, 34
PCs vs. Macs, 34
What's an Operating System?, 37
What Is a Compatible?, 40

6 Microprocessor and Memory, 42
The Microprocessor, 42
Memory, 47
The Motherboard, 49
Summary Checklist, 50

7 Disks, 52
Hard Drive, 52
Floppy Disks and Drives, 54
Other Drives, 56
Summary Checklist, 57

8 Other System Unit Considerations, 59
Expansion Slots, 59
Ports, 61
Power Supply, 62
Case Styles, 62
Summary Checklist, 63

9 Monitors, 65
Differences in Monitors, 65
Monitors and Adapters, 66
Resolution, 66
Monitor Standards, 67
Size, 68
Other Features, 68
Knobs and Swivels, 69
Summary Checklist, 70

10 Keyboard and Mouse, 72
Keyboards, 72
Mice, 74
Other Input Devices, 76

11 Printers, 78
Why Buy a Printer?, 78
Types of Printers, 78
Dot-Matrix Printers, 79
Inkjet Printers, 81
Laser Printers, 83
Summary Checklist, 84

12 Communications, 87
Understanding Communications, 87
Buying a Modem, 89
Buying a Fax Modem, 91
Selecting Software, 92
Hooking Up a Telephone Line, 93
Summary Checklist, 93

13 Multimedia PCs, 95
What Is Multimedia?, 95
Understanding the MPC Logo, 97
Buying a Multimedia PC, 98
Summary Checklist, 101

14 Other Equipment, 102
Furniture, 102
Supplies, 103
Summary Checklist, 104

15 Buying a Macintosh, 106
Macintosh Hardware, 106
Macintosh Software, 109
Macintosh Lines, 109

16 Buying a Portable Computer, 112
What Is a Portable Computer?, 112
Buying a Portable Computer, 114
Summary Checklist, 117

17 Completing Your Computer Shopping List, 119
Selecting Software, 119
Selecting Hardware, 120
Setting a Budget, 121
Summary Checklist, 121

18 Doing Some Research, 127
Reading Magazines, 127
Visiting Computer Stores, 130
Soliciting Advice from Others, 132

19 Deciding Where to Buy, 134
Where Computers Are Sold, 134
Computer Dealers, 134
Computer SuperStores, 135
Mail-Order Vendors, 136
Electronics Stores, 137
Department, Discount, and Office Supply Stores, 138
Local Box Makers, 138

20 Making the Purchase, 139
To Buy a Bundle or Not?, 139
Checking the Warranty, Service, and Support, 141
Comparing Systems, 142
Summary Checklist, 145

21 After the Sale, 147
Setting Up the Computer, 147
Do's and Don'ts, 149

Glossary, 153
Index, 161

Introduction

Buying a computer isn't an easy task. Computer stores and advertisements often bombard you with terms and acronyms you don't understand. Complete Multimedia package. 8MB RAM. 80486SX. 50MHz. CD-ROM. What does it all mean?

This book helps you make sense of all the terms and shows you how to make a smart purchase decision.

Welcome to Buying a Computer

You probably don't want to spend time reading 400-to-500-page books that tell you every detail about how a computer works and what you need to know about using a computer. You don't want to be an *expert* on computers; you just want to make a smart purchase decision. This book can help you do that.

First, this book focuses on the most critical factors in making a purchase decision. In advertisements, you see a lot of computer specifications (specs). This book helps you understand which ones are important and which ones aren't.

Second, the book explains terms in easy-to-understand language. You can easily make sense of the sales pitches after reading this book. No jargon!

Third, the book consists of short lessons; you should be able to read and understand the information in one lesson in 10 minutes or less.

Fourth, the book includes summary checklists so that you can record and keep track of what type of system you need.

Who Should Use Buying a Computer

Buying a Computer is for anyone who:

- Wants a simple guide that explains concepts so they are easy to understand.
- Doesn't have time to learn each and every specification of a computer.
- Feels overwhelmed by all the types of computers.
- Isn't sure what a computer can do or whether they need a computer.

How to Use This Book

Buying a Computer consists of a series of lessons. Each lesson helps you understand a key part of the purchase decision. You can read the lessons in order, or you can skip to the lessons that cover topics you have questions about. For example, you may know the type of computer you want, but may have trouble selecting a printer. If so, you can review the lesson on printers.

Icons Used in This Book

The following icons appear throughout the book to help you find your way around:

Timesaver Tips offer advice on how to save money or how to make the best decision.

Plain English definitions explain new terms.

Panic Button icons alert you to common mistakes or areas where you might have problems.

Acknowledgments

Thanks to Marie Butler-Knight, Publisher, for publishing this book; Barry Pruett, Acquisitions Manager, for signing the book; Faithe Wempen, Product Development Manager, for reviewing the outline and first chapter and making good suggestions; Liz Keaffaber, Managing Editor, and San Dee Phillips, Manuscript Editor, for handling the editing process; and Martha O'Sullivan, for handling all the paper processing and for always being so helpful.

Special thanks to Kelly Oliver, Development Editor, for her positive encouragement, insightful changes, and useful suggestions.

Lesson

Do I Need a Computer?

In this lesson, you will learn what a computer can and cannot do, and you will evaluate your reasons for purchasing a computer.

What Is a Computer?

A computer is an electronic appliance, such as a TV, VCR, or dryer, that you use to do something. The thrilling thing about computers is that you can use the computer to do many things. Unlike a washer that you use to do basically one thing (wash clothes), you can use your computer to write letters, draw a map, play a game, and much more.

What makes a computer so flexible is *software*, the programs or applications that you install and use on the computer. For instance, if you want to write a letter, you start and use word processing software. You will learn about software in more detail in this lesson and later lessons.

> **Software** Software are the programs that enable you to do different tasks on the computer. You may hear the term *application* or *program*, or some combination of the terms (software program, software application, application program); they all mean the same thing.

Hardware consists of the physical pieces of the computer, such as the monitor (TV-like component), system unit (the square box that the monitor sits on), and keyboard. When you purchase a new computer, be concerned about both the software and hardware that you select. There will be more details about hardware in the later lessons of this book.

What a Computer Can Do

Here are some of the things you can do on a computer:

- **Create documents.** Letters, memos, reports, newsletters, brochures, flyers, and more.

- **Work with figures.** Keep a budget, track your checkbook, track and total expenses, track sales information, figure loan costs, and so on.

- **Create drawings and pictures.** Create a logo, create charts, make simple drawings, design cards, design your dream home, and more.

- **Keep track of data.** Inventories, books, CDs, clients, projects, and so on.

- **Communicate with others.** Hook up to on-line services, such as Prodigy, CompuServe, and America Online, or the Internet to shop, play games, and talk with other on-line computer users.

- **Educate yourself.** Learn how to speak German, study astronomy, learn how to type, and more.

- **Have fun.** Fly a plane, drive a race car, be a detective—you can play just about any game you can think of.

The world of software is wide and diverse. If there's something you want to use your computer for, there's probably a software program to do it. The next lesson helps you match your needs to specific types of software programs. Here, you should just be familiar with all the possibilities.

Visit a Computer Store If you aren't sure what a computer can do, take a trip to a local computer store and browse around in the software section. Look at the different programs and what they can do. You can also get a good sense by reading the advertisements in computer magazines.

Benefits to Using a Computer

In addition to knowing what you want to do with the computer, you should also understand what benefits you hope to get from using a computer. Many people think that a computer is the answer to all problems. (With a computer, you can make more money, become more organized, save time, be more successful, and so on.) Before you purchase a computer, you should consider what the real benefits are, as well as the drawbacks.

Saving Time

Saving time is frequently mentioned as one of the benefits of using a computer. In many cases, you can save time. Here are some examples of what you can do with a computer:

- **Find information faster.** With a computer, you store the information you need on the computer; for example, your sales records. Rather than sort through paper records, you can quickly have the computer retrieve the information you need.

- **Reuse information.** If you repeatedly use the same information, such as a form letter, instead of having to retype the letter each time you need it, you can display and use the same letter again.

- **Have the computer do some of the work for you.** Many programs can do tasks much quicker than you can manually. For instance, suppose that you have 500 customer records and need to sort them. If you had to sort them by hand, who knows how long it would take. A computer can sort in a matter of seconds.

You need to offset the time you will save with the following factors:

- **Tinkering time.** You may be able to type a letter on the computer much faster and much more accurately. However, you will probably spend that saved time tinkering with the looks of the letter. Because it is easy to make changes, you may find yourself changing the margins, adding pictures, changing the typeface of the computer document—time you probably didn't spend when you used a typewriter.

- **Learning time.** When you first buy a computer, you are going to have to spend some time learning how to use it. At first, you may wish that you would have stuck with the manual method. Don't worry, though, your time investment will eventually pay off.

Being More Accurate

Another benefit of using a computer is that a computer can make your work more accurate. For example, if you type a letter, you can have the program check the spelling or grammar and then correct any errors. If you are figuring a budget, you can have the program calculate the totals. A computer won't make a mistake when adding a row of numbers.

The drawback to this benefit is that the computer is only as accurate as the person using it. This means that a computer won't total a column of numbers incorrectly, but if the person entering the numbers leaves one out or enters one incorrectly, the total may not be correct.

Being More Organized

Many new buyers want to purchase a computer to become more organized. And for good reason; a computer *can* make you more organized. Rather than store your contacts in an address book, you can store them on the computer and keep them up-to-date. Rather than keep a big filing cabinet with records, you can store the records electronically.

Keep in mind two points when considering this benefit. First, you will still need to work at being organized. If you don't update your contact information on the computer, it won't be accurate. If you don't follow a good organizational strategy for storing information on the computer, you won't be able to find it. Second, you may be able to cut down on the amount of paper information you keep, but you will not entirely eliminate paper copies.

Providing More Opportunities

One benefit that new users often don't consider is that a computer can provide you with more opportunities. Here are some examples:

- **Get a better understanding of your business.** Let's say, for example, that you own a small sales business. You bought a computer mainly to save time in keeping track of sales information, and you have saved *some* time, but not nearly as much as you expected. What you may not realize is how you can use the information you have to better manage your business. Manipulating information is easy with a computer, and you can manipulate the data to answer questions about your business. For example, what's your best-selling product? Who is your best client? What time of year are sales fast? Slow? Using this kind of information, you can make sure you service your best client well, plan promotions for slow times, and so on.

- **Do work at home.** If you don't have enough time in the office, you can purchase a home computer and do work at home. Being able to work in a more comfortable environment may help you be more productive.

- **Use the computer to start a new business.** For many purchasers, a computer opens up the opportunity for a new business. Perhaps, you want to start a medical transcription service or do bookkeeping from your home. You can use the computer as the basis for a new business.

- **Educate your children.** Many parents today feel that it is important for their children to learn how to use a computer—especially as computers and their use become more prevalent in the classroom.

Saving Money

Buying a computer to save money is probably the hardest benefit to justify. Usually the savings come in a roundabout way. For instance, you can argue that if you are saving time, you are saving money. You can use that saved time to make money. You can also save money if you use the computer to do work that you used to have to pay someone else to do. However, if you are doing the work, you are spending *your* time—so that may be a wash. If you want to buy a computer to save money, you should make sure that's not the only benefit you expect to gain.

Reasons You Want to Buy a Computer

Now that you have an understanding of what you can do with a computer and what the benefits are, make a list of *your* specific reasons for purchasing a computer. What do you want to do? What do you expect to gain? Use the summary checklist at the end of this lesson to help clarify your reasons. These reasons will help you better understand your computing needs. Once you understand what you want, you can find a computer to do just that.

Reasons Not to Buy a Computer

Just as there are many good reasons for buying a computer, there are also some bad reasons. If any of the following situations describes the reason(s) you want a computer, you should seriously consider whether you really need one:

- You want a computer because everyone else has one, and you think you need one, too.

- Computer prices are dropping, so you figure now is the best time to purchase one—even though you aren't sure what you will do with it.

- You figure that you'll decide how to use the computer after you buy it.

- You think it would be *neat* to have a computer. You don't want the computer age to pass you by.

Summary Checklist

Use this checklist to first list and then prioritize the reasons you want a computer. Understanding what you want is the first step in finding a computer to match your needs.

1. Check any of the following reasons you want a computer.

2. In the Priority column, rate the items you selected in step 1. Mark the most important benefit with 1, the next with 2, and so on.

Lesson 1

Important	Priority	Reason
❑	_____	Save time
❑	_____	Save money
❑	_____	Save myself some work
❑	_____	Expand my business
❑	_____	Do work at home
❑	_____	Educate my children
❑	_____	Be more organized
❑	_____	Be more accurate
❑	_____	Other _____
❑	_____	Other _____

Once you complete the list, you can refer to it when you decide what type of system and software you want.

Lesson 2

What Do I Want the Computer to Do?

In this lesson, you will learn about the different types of software, and you will make a software shopping list.

Software You Need

To use a computer, you need two kinds of software: an operating system and application software.

Operating System Software

Every computer has and comes with an operating system. Without an operating system, you wouldn't be able to do anything with the computer—even if you have application software. The operating system takes care of the basic tasks on the computer: displaying information on-screen, saving documents, finding and redisplaying documents, sending information to the printer, and much more.

Depending on the type of computer you purchase, your computer will use a specific operating system. IBMs and IBM-compatibles (one type of computer) usually use *Microsoft Windows*. Before 1995, IBM's and compatibles used DOS and Windows. But computers sold after August of 1995 probably come with the Windows 95 operating system, which does not require DOS as a user-friendly supplement to the operating system. Macintosh computers (another type of computer) use an operating system called the System. You can read more about operating systems in Lesson 5.

DOS and Windows *DOS* is an acronym for disk operating system. There are a few varieties of DOS, but MS-DOS (Microsoft Disk Operating System) is by far the most popular. Microsoft also manufactures a product called *Windows* that enables the user to navigate his system and issue commands by using icons (small pictures) and pull-down menus.

Application Software

In addition to operating system software, you also need application software. Depending on what you want to do, you will need different types of application software. Some companies design software to create documents or to create architectural drawings. The next sections describe the types of application software you can choose from.

Types of Application Software

There would be no way to list every type of software program available. For the most part, if there's something you want to do on the computer, you can usually find a program to do it. For example, there's software for drawing up a will, keeping track of recipes, charting your horoscope, tracking investments, and more. Here are the most common types of programs.

Word Processing Programs

If you want to create documents—letters, memos, reports, newsletters, manuscripts—you need a *word processing program*. A word processing program is the most commonly used application, and it does just what its name implies; it processes words.

You may think of a word processing program as a high-tech typewriter, but actually it is much more. Here are some of the things you can do with most word processing programs:

- **Easily change the text.** You can add text you forgot, delete text you don't need, move text to a new location, copy text, and more.

- **Change the appearance of text.** From adjusting the margins on the page to using indents to making text bold, you can change the appearance of text with formatting. Most word processing programs offer a rich variety of formatting features so that you can create anything from simple memos to complex annual reports.

- **Check for accuracy.** Most word processing programs contain a spelling program. This feature checks the words in your document against words in its dictionary and flags any words it can't find. You can then change or verify the words in the document. Some programs also offer a thesaurus and/or a grammar checker.

- **Save time.** Word processing programs also offer a variety of time-saving features. For instance, you can search quickly through a document to find a specific spot, and you can create form letters.

Figure 2.1 shows a sample document in a word processing program.

Lesson 2

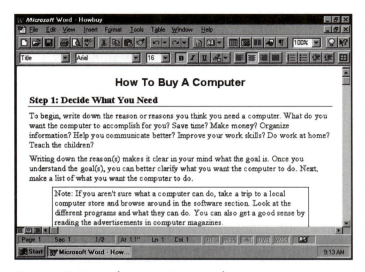

Figure 2.1 A document in a word processing program.

Spreadsheets and Other Financial Programs

Spreadsheets are the second most commonly used type of software. If you work with financial information (for example, track sales, figure budgets, or calculate loan amounts), you need a spreadsheet program.

In most spreadsheet programs, you enter the data in a *worksheet*: a grid of columns and numbers. You can then perform calculations on the data in the worksheet. Just like a word processing program is much more than a typewriter, a spreadsheet program is much more than a fancy calculator. Here are some of the things you can do with a spreadsheet program:

- **Perform simple to complex calculations.** In a worksheet, you can do simple equations, such as sum a row of numbers, and complex equations, such as figure the amount of return on an investment.

What Do I Want the Computer to Do?

- **Change the appearance of the data.** Just like a word processing program, you can format the data—add dollar signs, center an entry, make text bold, and so on.

- **Create a chart or graph.** Most spreadsheet programs include chart features so you can visually represent the data.

- **Manage data lists.** Although a spreadsheet program is not a database (see the next section), you can use this type of program to keep track of simple lists of information like client names or product information.

Figure 2.2 shows a worksheet and chart from a spreadsheet program.

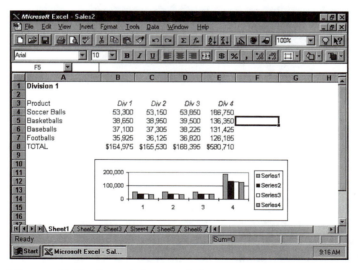

Figure 2.2 A worksheet and chart.

In addition to spreadsheet programs, you can also purchase and use other types of financial programs. For example, one of the most popular types of financial programs is a checkbook manager. You can use this program to track your savings, balance your account, and create tax reports. Figure 2.3 shows an example of this type of program.

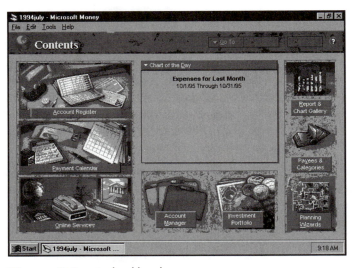

Figure 2.3 A checkbook program.

There are also sophisticated bookkeeping programs, tax preparation programs, and other types of financial software.

Database Programs

If you need to keep track of large amounts of information—clients, inventories, library information or sales—you need a *database program*. Database programs vary greatly, from a simple mailing-list program to a complex, linked system of information (for instance, all patients in a hospital with all their health and financial information).

Simple Needs? If your needs are simple, you may want to select a single-purpose database program, such as a mailing list program or a contact management program. Because these programs set up the database for you and include only the features applicable to that single purpose, they may be easier for you to use.

You can set up the database so that it contains fields (or blanks) for each piece of information you need. You can then quickly enter and manage the data. With a database program, you can search quickly to find the information you need. You can also sort information in different ways, for example, by last name or ZIP code in a client database. Finally, you can query the database; that is, ask it questions. For instance, you can create a query to show all the client bills over $500 and past 30 days due.

Graphics Programs

If you want to work with pictures—create a logo, draw a map, design a poster, work on a photograph—you will need some type of *graphics program*. This category is fairly broad and includes many different types of graphics programs. Here are some examples of the types of programs included in this category:

- **Presentation programs.** If you need to create a slide presentation, you can purchase a presentation program that will help you create, arrange, and output the presentation.

- **Painting programs.** Using a paint program, you can create simple pictures, as shown in Figure 2.4. Just as you draw on paper with pencils and pens, you similarly draw on-screen with the computer tools. The drawings consist of tiny elements called *pixels*. You can edit the individual pixels and change the drawing.

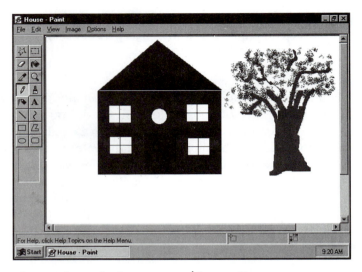

Figure 2.4 A picture created in a paint program.

- **Drawing programs.** A drawing program is similar to a paint program, only it uses a different method for creating the image. A drawn image does not consist of individual pixels; instead, it is defined as an object. You can change the size and shape of the object by changing the whole object.

- **CAD programs.** CAD stands for computer-aided design. You can use CAD programs to create architectural or manufacturing drawings or plans.

- **Sophisticated imaging and animation programs.** You can also use more sophisticated programs for manipulating computer images. You can scan in and then alter a photograph. You can create an animated cartoon.

Buy Clip Art If you can't draw, you can add drawings to your documents by using clip art. Clip art packages are predrawn images stored in electronic files that you can purchase and then use in your applications.

Communication Programs

To learn more about communicating with other computers or on-line services or the Internet, read Lesson 12. Keep in mind that in addition to needing special equipment, you also need software to communicate with other computers.

Integrated Programs

Many new computer systems come bundled with an *integrated program*. An *integrated program* is a combination of different types of programs all in one application. Most integrated programs contain simple word processing, spreadsheet, database, chart, drawing, and communication programs.

The plus side of integrated programs is they are simple; you have to learn only one program. On the down side, the programs don't offer as many features as single-purpose packages. For example, an integrated package will have some simple formatting features, while a word processing package will have many formatting features.

Desktop Publishing Programs

If you want to create sophisticated documents (beyond the capabilities of your word processing program), you need a *desktop publishing program*. With desktop publishing programs, you can easily work with and lay out text and graphics on the page. For example, you can create a newsletter or design a brochure.

Educational and Recreational Programs

Probably one of the widest areas of software programs is the educational and recreational category. You can find programs that teach you anything: typing, cooking, fixing up your home, planning your wedding, tracing your family tree, fixing your car, and so on. Children can learn reading, math, anatomy, geography, and more using computer programs.

For games, you can build your own city, fight an evil dragon, fly an airplane, race a car, or play golf, baseball, basketball, chess, solitaire, or football. If you have a hobby or interest, there's likely to be a software program designed for you.

Utility Programs

The final category of software is *utility programs*. These are programs you can use to better manage your computer. You can get back files you've accidentally deleted with an Undelete utility. You can use other utilities to make your computer work at its optimal condition.

Deciding What You Want to Do

Now that you are aware of all the possibilities, make a list of what you would like to do on the computer. You can write out the list or use the summary checklist at the end of this lesson.

To get ideas, think of how you do things now (manually). Then think about whether you could do them on the computer. Be sure to put as many items as you want on the list. Think not just how you will use the computer today, but how you will use it next year and the year after that. If you buy a computer that meets only what you want today, you may not be satisfied later on.

Who Else Will Use the Computer?

As you make your list, consider also who else will use the computer. Will your spouse also use the computer? Will your children? If others will use the computer, be sure to include their needs in your software shopping list.

What Software Do You Use Now?

If you already have and use a computer (perhaps at work), be sure to note the type of software you use. If, for example, you use a spreadsheet program at work and want to be able to do this type of work at home, you will need a spreadsheet program (probably the same program that you use at work).

Summary Checklist

When you purchase a computer, this list will help you describe exactly what you want to do. This list will also be useful when you need to decide which software programs you need to purchase.

1. Check all the things you want to do with the computer. If several people will use the computer, you may want to have each person complete his or her own list.

2. Prioritize the list, marking the most important task with 1, the next important task with 2, and so on.

I want to be able to...	Type of Program	Priority
❑ Create letters, memos, reports, and other documents.	Word processing	_____
❑ Work with numbers: total sales, set up a budget, figure loan payments.	Spreadsheet	_____
❑ Keep track of my checking account, investments, budget.	Financial	_____
❑ Keep track of sets of data: inventory, books, clients.	Database	_____

Lesson 2

- [ ] Use a single, simple package to create letters, work with numbers, and keep track of data.   Integrated   _____

- [ ] Create simple pictures.   Paint   _____

- [ ] Create sophisticated drawings or logos.   Draw   _____

- [ ] Create detailed architectural or mechanical drawings.   CAD   _____

- [ ] Create a slide show for a presentation.   Presentation   _____

- [ ] Create sophisticated documents: newsletters, brochures, and more.   Desktop publishing   _____

- [ ] Communicate with other computers.   Communication   _____

- [ ] Have fun: fly a plane, drive a race car, hunt for hidden treasure, and more!   Recreational   _____

- [ ] Learn something new: learn Spanish, improve my typing.   Educational   _____

- [ ] Tweak and maintain my computer system: maximize my hard disk size, undelete files.   Utility   _____

- [ ] Other _____

Lesson 3

How to Select Software

In this lesson, you will learn how to select a software package and review the system requirements for that package.

Picking a Software Package

If you needed a word processing program and there was only one, the purchase decision would be easy. However, for most categories of software, there are many packages available, and selecting the "right" one can be difficult. First, most programs are comparable. They offer similar features and prices. Second, there's no clear-cut way of determining which is the "best" product. If you ask three people which is the best word processing program, you may get three different answers. You have to decide what's best for *you*.

> **Software in a Bundle** If you need several programs, consider buying a software bundle, such as Microsoft Office. This package provides several separate, popular software programs in one package at a reasonable price. These packages are a good deal if you need all the programs. If you will use only one program, though, you don't need a bundle.

To help you make your decision, consider using one of the following strategies:

- **Take the software provided with the computer system.** Many computer systems come bundled with software programs. If these programs suit your needs, you may not need to look any further for software.

- **Use the same software you use in your office.** If you are using a computer in your office and want to do work at home, you may want to purchase and use the same software on your home computer. You don't *have to* select the same software, but doing so may make working at home easier. You won't have to learn two programs, and you won't have to worry about transferring files from one program to another.

- **Ask the software salesperson to recommend a particular package.** Don't just take his answer at face value: Quiz him about why he made the recommendation. Why is this package better than another? What are the differences between two packages? You can also ask friends, coworkers, and relatives to make recommendations. Also, find out what other people in your business use.

- **Try out the different packages.** Most computer stores allow you to demo the software. After you try the programs, pick the one you are most comfortable with. Use this strategy particularly when you want to use a special feature of the program. Most programs operate in a similar fashion. However, when you get into specialized features, such as equations, one program may be easier to use than another.

How to Select Software

- **Buy the most inexpensive software.** If price concerns you the most, you may want to let the cost of the software dictate your decision. However, be sure that you get a program that has all the features you need. You won't save any money if you select a "cheap" program now and then need to upgrade to a more full-featured program later.

> **Going Out of Business!** Make sure that the software you select is going to be available for a while. You don't want to standardize on Word-o-Matic for your office if Word-o-Matic is going out of business. You want a company with a commitment to support and upgrade the product.

Some Popular Programs

This section lists some of the most popular programs within a category. Most programs become popular because they offer a good feature set for a good price. Therefore, you can pretty much buy any of the programs listed and not have too many problems or complaints.

> **Where's the One I Want?** Keep in mind that just because you don't see a product listed here doesn't mean it isn't a worthwhile product. This list just gives you some ideas.

Word Processing

Word (Microsoft Corporation) Offered in Windows, DOS, and Mac versions and included in Microsoft Office.

WordPerfect (WordPerfect Corporation) Offered in Windows, DOS, and Mac versions and often used in the legal field. Included in Perfect Office.

Ami Pro (Lotus Corporation) Only available in a Windows version and included in Lotus SmartSuite.

Spreadsheet

Excel (Microsoft Corporation) Available in Windows and Mac versions and included in Microsoft Office.

1-2-3 (Lotus Corporation) Offered in DOS, Windows, and Mac versions and included in Lotus SmartSuite.

Financial

Quicken (Intuit) Offered in Windows and DOS versions.

Money (Microsoft Corporation) Available only in a Windows version.

Integrated

Works (Microsoft Corporation) Available in DOS, Windows, and Mac versions.

ClarisWorks (Claris Corporation) Available in Windows and Mac versions.

Database

Access (Microsoft Corporation)   Available only in a Windows version: a full-featured database program.

Paradox (Borland)   Offered in Windows and DOS versions: a full-featured database.

Graphics

CorelDRAW! (Corel)   Offered only in a Windows version: a full-featured chart, draw, and paint program.

Paint (Microsoft Corporation)   A simple paint program included with Microsoft Windows 95.

PowerPoint (Microsoft Corporation)   Sold in Windows and Mac versions: a presentation program included in Microsoft Office.

Freelance Graphics (Lotus Corporation)   Available in a Windows version: a presentation program included in Lotus SmartSuite.

Harvard Graphics (SPC)   Offered in DOS and Windows versions: a presentation program.

PrintShop (Broderbund)   Available in DOS, Windows, and Mac versions: a popular, easy-to-use program for creating posters, cards, brochures, and so on.

Decoding the Software Requirements

To operate, all software requires certain minimum hardware standards. You can often find these standards listed on the box under the heading "System Requirements." The following shows a typical system requirement listing from a software package.

System Requirements:

- Microsoft Windows 3.1 or later
- PC with 80486 or higher microprocessor
- 4MB of system memory and 5MB of free hard disk space
- Mouse or other Windows-compatible pointing device (optional)
- Hayes- or 100%-compatible modem required for auto-dialing

Why Read the Requirements?

For the most part, you should buy a system powerful enough to run most application programs so you don't have to worry too much about the requirements. Still, you should check the requirements for these reasons:

- Read the requirements of the software you want to use to get a general idea of the minimum system you will require.

- If you are selecting a particularly complex program, such as a CAD program, you should check the system requirements carefully. Because these requirements are more demanding, you may need to select a more high-powered system to run this type of software.

- When purchasing new software, read the requirements to be sure you have all the equipment you need, such as a modem or mouse.

What the Requirements Mean

The following list summarizes the information usually included in the system requirements section. For more information on hardware (concepts such as memory and hard disk space), turn to the later lessons in the book.

Most system requirements include the following:

- **Required operating system**   This lists the type of operating system you must have (for instance, DOS) and the version (for example, 5.0 or higher).

- **Microprocessor**   This lists the microprocessor you must have. Note that sometimes the system requirements will list the minimum and recommended microprocessor. This means that the program will run on the minimum chip, but probably very slowly. You should get the recommended microprocessor. (You can read about microprocessors in Lesson 6.)

- **Memory**   The amount of memory you need listed in megabytes (M or MB). You can read more about memory in Lesson 6. Keep in mind that memory is a temporary working area. If you have two programs and one requires 2MB and another requires 4MB, that doesn't mean you need a total of 6MB. You need just the largest amount (4MB).

- **Hard disk space**   The amount of hard disk space you need listed in megabytes (M or MB). Hard disk space is permanent storage, meaning that if one program requires 5MB and another requires 10MB, both programs together require 15MB.

> **Remember!**   Many beginners confuse memory and disk space. *Memory* is a temporary storage place (see Lesson 6). *Hard disk space* is permanent storage space (see Lesson 7).

- **Other equipment**   If you need other equipment, such as a mouse or modem, you can find that information also. Sometimes, you will see the type of monitor you need listed as well.

Other Things to Check

When you are reading the requirements, you can probably tell whether the software is for an IBM, IBM-compatible (PC), or a Macintosh computer (Mac). Still, if you aren't sure, check the package. Many programs come in both formats, and you can use the format for your computer type only. For instance, if you have a PC, you can't use software designed for the Mac. (Lesson 5 covers the differences between PCs and Macs.)

Another thing to check is the disk size. Most programs come on 3 1/2-inch disks or CD-ROMs. (You can read more about disks in Lesson 7.) Be sure to get the disk size that matches your computer's disk drives.

Summary Checklist

Use this form to record the software requirements for each type of program you want to purchase. If you need to make notes for several programs, make a copy for each program you need to check.

Software program
_____

Operating system required
_____

Processor required
_____

Amount of memory
_____

How to Select Software

Amount of hard disk space
_____

Type of monitor
_____

Other requirements
_____

Type of disk
_____

Lesson 4

Understanding Computers

This lesson briefly explains how a computer works and describes the parts that make up a computer.

What Is Hardware?

Hardware consists of the physical components that make up the computer system: the pieces that you can see and touch. All computer systems have these three basic parts:

- **System Unit**   This box-like component stores the electronic parts of the computer. Inside this box, you will find the microprocessor, memory chips, power supply, and disk drives. Lessons 6, 7, and 8 cover these topics in more detail.

- **Monitor**   This TV-like component displays on-screen what you type on the keyboard. The monitor connects to the system unit via a cable. You can read more about monitors in Lesson 9.

- **Keyboard**   This typewriter-like thing is what you use to type commands and enter information. Lesson 10 explains the keyboard in more detail.

Your computer may also have equipment such as a mouse, modem, or printer. This additional equipment is also hardware.

How a Computer Works

You may wonder how the pieces of hardware work together. In simple terms, here's how:

1. **Input.** You enter data or a command using an input device, such as the keyboard or mouse.

2. **Processing.** The computer (the parts inside the system unit) processes the information—it does what you tell it to do.

3. **Output.** The information appears on-screen or is printed.

Input and output are fairly simple to understand because you can *see* the results. As you type (input), you see the characters on-screen (output). The real "magic" occurs inside the system unit.

There you find the electronic components that make up a computer. (Lesson 6 and 7 describe the system unit components in more detail.). The main component, called the *microprocessor*, is a small chip about the size of a cracker. On this chip, there are millions of tiny switches called *transistors*.

You can turn each individual switch on or off. The computer uses a binary numbering system to represent the on (1) or off (0) stage of the switch. Because it would be impossible to represent information with just two switches, the computer combines a series of on and off switches into a byte (a series of eight switches). One byte can represent, for example, one letter. 01000001 represents the letter A; 01000010 represents the letter B, and so on.

It takes a person a while to process 01000001, but the computer can process this information—and much more—in a fraction of a second. That's the magic of computing.

A Personal Computer Timeline

One of the founders of the first microprocessor company came up with Moore's Law. This law states that the number of transistors on a computer chip will double every 18 months. That means that every 1 1/2 years or so a new computer may appear that is twice as powerful as its predecessor.

To give you an idea of how far personal computers have come in just a short time, review the following timeline:

1975   A hobbyist creates the first personal computer called the Altair 8800. This hobbyist, a doctor, offers to sell kits through *Popular Electronics* magazine. The computer is a box that you program by flipping switches on the front panel. Other hobbyists and early computer enthusiasts become intrigued.

1976   Steve Wozniak and Steve Jobs build the Apple I, another type of personal computer. This computer still has no keyboard, case, sound, or graphics. (The Apple eventually evolved into the Macintosh computers of today.)

1981   IBM debuts its personal computer. This computer has a monitor, keyboard, and system unit. This computer uses an 8088 chip that has 29,000 transistors. IBM makes the hardware design available to other developers so that they can write software. Bill Gates, the founder of Microsoft, introduces MS-DOS.

1982 — IBM clones (or compatibles) appear on the market. These personal computers work the same way and run the same software as IBM computers.

1984 — Apple introduces the Macintosh computer. IBM rolls out the AT which includes an 80286 microprocessor. This microprocessor has 130,000 transistors.

1988 — Compaq beats IBM to market with the first 80386 computer. The 80386 chip has 275,000 transistors.

1990 — Microsoft Corporation introduces Windows. The 80486 chip appears. This chip has 1.2 million transistors.

1993 — The Pentium (or 586) chip enters the marketplace. This chip has 3.1 million transistors.

1994 — The PowerPC chip arrives. This chip uses a different method for processing data and is very fast.

1995 — Development begins on the next generation of Pentiums—P6 or 686. This processor has 5.5 million transistors.

Windows 95 introduced.

Now that you understand how a computer works and how computer technology has developed, you can better understand the individual hardware components that make up a computer. In the next lesson, you'll learn the differences between computers.

Lesson 5

Types of Computers

In this lesson, you will learn the differences between PCs and Macintoshes, and their different operating systems.

Summarizing the Differences

Understanding the differences between the types of computers can be confusing. What's a PC? What's a compatible? Are Macs and PCs the same? Computers differ in three basic ways:

First, there are two types of computers: IBMs and compatibles (referred to as PCs) and Macintoshes (called Macs). The section "PCs vs. Macs" covers the differences between these two types of computers in detail.

Second, there are different types of operating systems. The Mac uses only one operating system, and the PC can use one of several. The section on operating systems can help you compare the operating systems.

Third, there are different categories of PCs: IBM PCs (manufactured and sold by IBM) and IBM-compatibles (computers manufactured by other companies). The section "What Is a Compatible?" defines what compatible means.

PCs vs. Macs

As mentioned, there are two main types of computers: PCs and Macs. In many ways, the two types of computers are similar:

- Their function is the same: you can use both to run any of the applications mentioned previously (word processing programs, spreadsheets, and so on), and most popular software packages come in both a PC and a Mac version.

- The two computers operate in a similar fashion: input, processing, and output.

- A PC and Mac are both composed of the same hardware components (system unit, monitor, and keyboard).

Understanding the Differences

What's the difference then? A PC and a Mac differ in these ways:

- The types of components used inside the system unit are different. For example, the Mac uses a different type of microprocessor.

- Because the types of computers use different components, you can't use Macintosh parts on a PC and vice versa.

- You also cannot use PC software on a Mac or Mac software on a PC. You have to buy a version of the software specific to the type of computer you have.

- Without special software, you cannot use a Macintosh disk with a PC.

- There are many more manufacturers of PCs.

- Macintosh computers and PCs use a different operating system; therefore, they differ somewhat in how you use them. The "What's an Operating System?" section later in this chapter discusses operating systems in more detail.

Deciding Between the Two

Your first main decision then becomes whether you should purchase a PC or a Macintosh computer. That's not an easy decision. If you talk to someone that uses a Macintosh, she will probably tell you the Macintosh is the better computer. If you talk to a PC person, he will probably insist a PC is a better deal.

To help you make this decision, consider the following points:

- If you use one type of computer at the office or if your children are using one type of computer at school, you will probably want to purchase the same type of computer. For instance, if you use a PC in the office, get a PC for the home. If you mix the types (have a Mac at one place and a PC at another), you will have to learn how to use two separate types of computers, and you will have to use special software to be able to use Mac information on the PC and vice versa.

- If you don't have access to another computer and want the most popular type of computer, buy a PC. Around 3/4 of all computers sold in the U.S. are PCs. This is the main reason you should consider a PC; more people and businesses have and use a PC.

- If computers intimidate you, if compatibility is not a concern, and you want the easiest computer to learn and use, buy a Macintosh. For the most part, a Macintosh computer is easier to use.

- There are many manufacturers of PCs, but only one manufacturer of Mac computers. Because the competition in the PC market is stiffer, you may get a better price for a PC. Recently though, Apple has responded to the pricing changes in the PC market by introducing competitively priced Macintoshes.

- You can easily add equipment to either the Mac or the PC, but there are some differences. Because the PC is so popular, many companies manufacture products (software and hardware) designed to work on the PC. You may have a wider selection. Because the PC uses an *open architecture*, there won't be set standards on how to connect hardware to the system unit, so you may have a hard time getting the equipment hooked up and working.

  The Mac, on the other hand, uses a *closed architecture*. Apple manufactures most parts and software. If a third party does create a product for the Mac, it must conform to rigorous standards. This means that you aren't likely to find as many manufacturers of Macintosh add-on products. However, when you do want to add something, hooking up the equipment is easier because the equipment has to follow strict standards.

- In the past, Macintosh computers had better graphics capability. Therefore, if you wanted to do intense desktop publishing or if you worked with complex graphics (such as photographs or four-color designs), you'd most likely want a Macintosh. Today, the PC has caught up in graphics capability, so if you want to do this same type of work, you can buy a PC.

Note that most lessons in this book focus mainly on PC hardware. If you want to purchase a Macintosh computer, be sure to review Lesson 15, which covers buying a Macintosh.

What's an Operating System?

As mentioned in Lesson 2, all computers need an operating system to work. The main difference you will notice when comparing a Mac and a PC is the operating system.

PC Operating Systems

Before 1995, most PCs used an operating system called DOS. This operating system is cryptic and difficult to use. All you see on-screen is a prompt (see Figure 5.1). To get the computer to do something, you have to type a command in the exact format required.

Figure 5.1 The DOS prompt.

To make the computer easier to use, the makers of MS-DOS (the most popular version of DOS) created an additional program to work on top of DOS. This program, called Microsoft Windows, uses icons (small pictures) to represent programs and documents. Microsoft Windows is a *GUI*. Windows makes it easier to use the computer because you can point at what you want with the mouse instead of having to remember DOS command names and syntax. Figure 5.2 shows a screen from Microsoft Windows 95.

What's a GUI? Microsoft Windows is a GUI (pronounced "GOO-ey"). GUI stands for graphical user interface and means the program uses graphics to represent elements on-screen.

Types of Computers 39

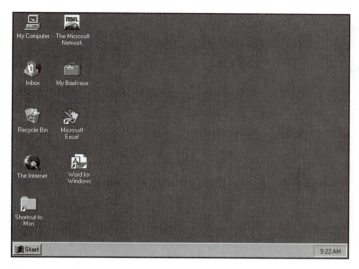

Figure 5.2 Microsoft Windows 95.

In 1995 Microsoft introduced a new version of Windows called Windows 95. This version incorporates the function of DOS into Windows. When you start the computer, you no longer see the DOS prompt. Instead, Windows starts automatically (see Figure 5.2). This new version of Windows 95 offers many advantages over the previous versions. One of the biggest benefits is a technology called Plug and Play which makes it easier to add new hardware to your system.

Most computers sold at the end of 1995 included Windows 95. When you purchase a computer, you need to be sure you are getting Windows 95 and not the older version.

The Macintosh Operating System

The Macintosh computer, on the other hand, has always used a graphical interface and, therefore, has always been easy to use. Figure 5.3 shows a picture of the Macintosh desktop.

System is the name of the Macintosh operating system.

Lesson 5

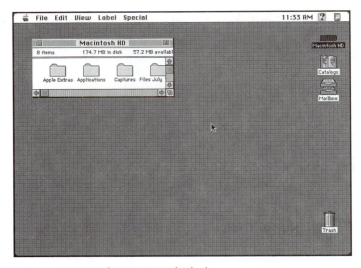

Figure 5.3 The Macintosh desktop.

What Is a Compatible?

If you decide to buy a PC, you must decide whether you want an IBM computer or a compatible. IBM dominated the mainframe (big computer) market when personal computers first appeared. The company saw the growing interest in the personal computer and quickly introduced the IBM PC. Because IBM was in a hurry to get the computer to the market, they created an open design or open architecture. They used chips created by one company, a hard drive created by another company, and an operating system by another. Using technology developed and created by other companies enabled them to create the first IBM PC very quickly. And the IBM PC became the industry standard.

The open architecture also enabled others to copy the design. It was only a matter of time before another company put together a PC using chips from one company, a hard drive from another, and so on. The industry calls these clones *IBM-compatibles*. The term *PC* generically refers to

Types of Computers

any IBM or IBM-type computer. There are probably 40 or so major manufacturers of PCs in the U.S. In the past, it was sometimes risky to buy a clone because some of them were not as reliable as the real IBMs. However, thanks to technology and experience, major PC manufacturers now produce quality machines at reasonable prices. There is no real difference between an IBM computer and an IBM-compatible.

A new computer chip introduced in 1994, called the PowerPC, enables you to use both Mac and PC software on the same machine. Lesson 6 covers this new development.

In this lesson, you learned about the differences between different types of computers. In the next lesson, you'll learn about microprocessors and memory.

Lesson 6

The Microprocessor and Memory

In this lesson, you will learn about two key elements that determine a computer's power: the microprocessor and memory.

The Microprocessor

The most important part of a computer is the *microprocessor chip*, sometimes called the CPU (central processing unit) or simply processor. This tiny chip the size of a cracker determines the power of a computer.

The two most important distinctions of the microprocessor are the name or type of chip and the speed. If you have looked at a computer advertisement, you probably noticed information like this in the ads:

P5/100MHz

The first bit of information (P5) is the name or type of chip. The second bit of information is the speed (100MHz). In addition to these critical pieces of information, you may also see the type of bus (ISA or EISA). This section describes the type, speed, and bus type of microprocessor chips. (For information on Macintosh microprocessors, see Lesson 15.)

The Type of Chip

Numbers denote the power of processor chips. The higher the number, the more powerful the chip. Remember

The Microprocessor and Memory

Moore's Law: every 18 months a new chip appears that is twice as powerful as its predecessor. The new chip is the king of the hill: the most powerful and most expensive. The chip that was the king (the next powerful) drops in price, and the chip that was second drops to third and borders on obsolescence.

Here is a breakdown of the different chips:

Chip	Pronounced	Description
8088	eighty eighty-eight	Used in the original IBM PC. Now obsolete.
8086	eighty eighty-six	Used in the IBM PC XT. Now obsolete.
80286	two eighty-six	Used in the AT computers introduced in 1984. Now obsolete.
80386	three eighty-six	A fairly powerful chip that can run Windows. Now obsolete.
80486	four eighty-six	Introduced in 1991. This chip was the top-of-the-line until the Pentium appeared.
Pentium	Pentium	Basically, a 80586 chip. Intel, the manufacturer of the chips, broke tradition and didn't name the chip with a number. This is the current top-of-the-line chip and appears in the most expensive computer systems.

continues

Lesson 6

Continued

Chip	Pronounced	Description
P6	P6	The next chip is called the P6, which is basically a 686. You can expect systems using this chip to be introduced in early 1996. This chip will then be the top-of-the-line, and the Pentium will be the second fastest.
PowerPC	PowerPC	A new type of chip that uses a different method for processing data. This chips enables you to use both Mac and PC software on the same computers.

SX, DX, Etc.

In addition to the chip number, you may see SX or DX. SX indicates the processor isn't as powerful as the regular chip (think standard). It doesn't include a *math coprocessor*.

The 386SX is a scaled-down and cheaper version of the 386 chip, while the 486SX chip is exactly the same as a 486DX chip except it doesn't have the math coprocessor. (Most people can get along fine without the math coprocessor.)

Math Coprocessor A math coprocessor is an additional chip that speeds up performing certain mathematical functions. The 486DX has a math coprocessor included. The SX does not. All Pentium and P6 computers come with a math coprocessor. If you do intense graphics work or a lot of complex spreadsheet calculations, you may want a math coprocessor.

DX indicates the full-fledged or deluxe chip. DX2 means the chip is twice as fast as the rest of the computer. DX4 means the chip is three times as fast.

Speed

In addition to deciphering the name, you also have to understand the *speed*. Manufacturers rate the speed of the chip in megahertz (MHz). One megahertz equals one million clock ticks per second. The higher the megahertz, the faster the computer.

Most chips are available in different speeds, and you will pay more for the faster computer. The following table gives you examples of different chips and the speeds available, from least powerful to most powerful.

Chip	Speed (in MHz)
8088	4.77
8086	8
80286	6-12
80386SX	20, 25
80386DX	25, 33, 40
80486SX	25, 33
80486DX	25, 33, 50
80486DX2	50, 66
80486DX2	100
Pentium	75, 100, 120, 133
P6	150+

Bus

The different components of the system unit connect electronically. This electronic pathway is the *bus*, and different computers use different buses.

First, buses differ in the amount of information they can move along the path. Some buses have 16 paths called 16-bit buses (think of 16 lanes on a highway). Some buses have 32 paths called 32-bit buses (think of 32 lanes on a highway). The more paths, the faster the computer can move information.

Second, buses conform to different standards. The most common standards are ISA (Industry Standard Architecture), EISA (Extended Industry Standard Architecture), and MCA (Micro Channel Architecture).

EISA buses are the most powerful; they are 32-bit buses. Commonly used ISA are 16-bit buses. You will only find MCA buses in IBM computers.

The latest in buses are the VESA (or VL bus) and the PCI bus. Manufacturers designed the VESA (Video Electronics Standards Association) to run at a faster rate than the ISA bus. It is inexpensive and provides better performance than the ISA bus. Because this bus appeared before the PCI bus, it has gained a good deal of market share. The second version of this bus is the VL2.

The PCI (Peripheral Component Interconnect) bus appeared after the VESA bus. This bus offers a 32-bit path between the CPU and peripherals and is backward compatible to ISA devices. This bus offers more features and will be able to work with newer microprocessor chips.

Buses also apply to expansion cards (covered in Lesson 8) and video cards (covered in Lesson 9).

What Bus Do I Need? Deciding which bus to get is a pretty technical decision. For the long range, you may want to buy the newest technology: the PCI bus. Doing so will ensure you aren't lagging behind the technology.

Manufacturers

You may have seen commercials for Intel on TV where you fly through the insides of a computer. Intel doesn't make computers; they make the microprocessor chip used inside the computer. As you now know, this chip is the most critical part of the computer.

For a long time, Intel dominated the PC chip market, but now there is competition. You may see other chip-makers used, such as Advanced Micro Devices (AMD). Be sure that the chip has been tested and that the company is going to support that chip. You don't want to purchase a chip from a fly-by-night chip maker.

Pass the Chips! As a beginner, stick with an Intel chip.

Memory

After the microprocessor, the next most important part of the computer is the amount of memory it has. A computer has two types of memory: *RAM* and *ROM*.

RAM

RAM stands for random access memory and is the working area where the computer stores instructions and data. The bigger the working area (more memory), the better.

RAM holds *bytes* of data. Computers sold today come with a range of 640K (640 kilobytes) to 16M (16 megabytes) of memory. Sometimes, you may see "4M expandable to

8M." That means the computer normally comes with 4M, but you can purchase the computer with 8M (or add up to 8M later). The more memory you have, the more expensive the computer.

> **Byte** One kilobyte (abbreviated K or KB) equals roughly 1,000 bytes. One megabyte (abbreviated M or MB) equals 1,000,000 bytes. One gigabyte (abbreviated G or GB) equals 1 billion bytes.

When you purchase a computer, you want to be sure of the following:

- Get as much memory as you can. You can probably get by with 8M, but 16M is better.

- Check the system requirements for the programs you want to run. These requirements will list the minimum amount of memory required.

- Be sure to inquire about adding memory. Make sure that you can easily add memory to the computer if you choose to do so later.

> **Buy As Much Memory As You Can!**
> Memory is one feature worth spending extra money on. You can never have enough memory. So if you are deciding whether to purchase extra memory or some other option, get the extra memory.

ROM

In addition to RAM, a computer also has *ROM*, or read-only memory. ROM chips contain the BIOS (Basic Input/Output System) and other critical information you need to start and use your computer. The information in ROM is hard-coded on the chip; that is, you cannot change it.

> **BIOS** Stands for basic input/output system. This software manages the communication between the hardware.

For the most part, you don't have to worry about the size or type of ROM chips when you purchase a computer.

Cache

The computer can use some tricks to make it work faster, and one such trick is the use of a *disk cache* (pronounced "cash"). The computer makes some assumptions about the information you use. If it thinks you are going to need certain information again, it stashes the information in a spot where the computer can quickly access it: in the cache. The larger the cache size, the more information it can store. You will see cache sizes advertised from 8K to 256K. A cache is important, but not critical, to your purchase decision.

The Motherboard

The microprocessor, memory, and expansion slots are located on one circuit board called the *motherboard* (see Figure 6.1). You already know about the microprocessor and memory. Lesson 8 covers the power supply and expansion slots.

Lesson 6

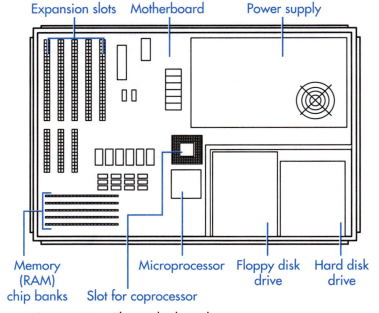

Figure 6.1 The motherboard.

Summary Checklist

Use this checklist to note the processor type, processor speed, and amount of memory you want.

1. Check the type of processor you want:

    ❑ 80486DX

    ❑ 80486DX2

    ❑ 80486DX4

    ❑ Pentium

The Microprocessor and Memory

2. Check the processor speed you want:
- ❏ 75
- ❏ 100
- ❏ 120
- ❏ 133

3. Check the amount of memory you need:
- ❏ 4M
- ❏ 8M
- ❏ 16M
- ❏ 32M

Lesson

Disks

In this lesson, you learn about disk drives: why you need them and what type you need.

Hard Drive

A major component of the system unit is the hard drive. A hard drive enables you to permanently store your data and your programs.

Many people confuse a hard drive with memory. It's important that you keep the two separate in your mind. Memory is only a temporary holding spot. You may want to think of memory as counter space. When you want to cook something, you get out all the things you need and put them on the counter. You can only fit a certain amount of items on the counter, but you can also put away items you don't need and then get out items you do need.

You can think of a hard drive as a cabinet: the place where you keep things you aren't working on right now. You usually have a lot more cabinet room than you do counter space.

Hard Drive Sizes

Like memory, hard drives are measured in bytes: megabytes (M or MB) and gigabytes (G or GB). Also, like memory, you want to get as big a hard drive as you can afford. Common hard disk sizes range from 100MB to 1G+.

Disks 53

Recommended Hard Disk Size You probably want to get at least an 800MB hard drive or bigger. You may think that you don't have much to store now, but you will quickly fill up your hard disk.

If you need more space, you can add extra hard drives, either inside the system unit or outside of it. Plus, there is software available that enables you to squeeze more information on the drive. This type of software is a disk compression program; the most popular program is Stacker. Another is DriveSpace, which comes with DOS.

Speed of Hard Drives

The industry rates hard drives by how long the hard drives take (in milliseconds, or ms) to find and retrieve information. The lower the number, the faster the drive. Speeds range from 20ms to 10ms. Speed isn't a critical decision factor, as long as you get a drive within this 20–10ms range.

Types of Hard Drive Controllers

The microprocessor and hard drive connect via a controller, and there are different types of controllers:

Name	Stands for	Description
EIDE	Enhanced Integrated Device Electronics	Newest controller. Buy this type to get the latest technology.
IDE	Integrated Device Electronics	Acceptable, high-speed controller.
ESDI	Enhanced Small Device Interface	Acceptable, high-speed controller.
MFM	Modified Frequency Modulation	Out-of-date standard.

Name	Stands for	Description
SCSI	Small Computer Systems Interface	Acceptable, high-speed controller. This type of controller enables you to chain (connect) different devices together and is more expensive.

Floppy Disks and Drives

Floppy drives are also stored inside the system unit. These drives enable you to put information onto the hard drives, such as a program, and to move information from the hard disk to the floppy disk. For example, if you want to work on a document that you created in your office, you can copy the disk from your office hard drive to a floppy disk. At home, you can then copy the same document from the floppy disk to the hard drive on your home computer.

With a hard drive, the disk and drive are one unit. You may hear the terms *hard disk*, *hard drive*, and *hard disk drive*. They all mean the same thing. With a floppy drive, you have two separate parts: the drive itself and the disk.

How a Floppy Drive Works

The drive is stored inside a bay in the system unit. You can insert disks into the drive via the slots on the front of the computer. There are two sizes of drives: 5 1/4-inch drives and 3 1/2-inch drives.

The 5 1/4-inch drives have a latch (see fig. 7.1). You insert the disk into the computer and then flip the latch. The 3 1/2-inch disks don't have a latch. When you insert this type of disk, an eject button pops out of the drive. You can eject the disk by pressing this button. (Some newer 5 1/4-inch drives also have a button.)

Disks 55

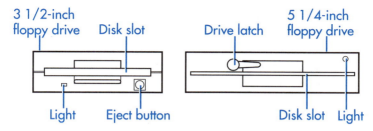

Figure 7.1 Floppy drives.

All computers have at least one floppy drive; some may have two, one of each size. What you need will depend on what types of disks you need to access. See the next section.

Floppy Disks

Each type of floppy drive uses a matching type of floppy disk: 3 1/2-inch drives use 3 1/2-inch disks, and 5 1/4-inch drives use 5 1/4-inch disks (see Figure 7.2).

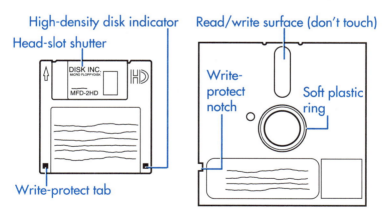

Figure 7.2 Floppy disks.

The disks not only vary in size, they also look different. The 3 1/2-inch disk is encased in a hard plastic coating. Even though it feels hard, it is still a floppy disk. The 5 1/4-inch disk is more flexible and may seem more like a "floppy" disk.

Floppy disks also vary in the amount of information they can store. The capacity is the amount of information a disk can store, and kilobytes (K or KB) and megabytes (M or MB) are the measurement of the capacity. Older 5 1/4-inch disks stored 360K and are known as double-density disks. Newer high-density 5 1/4-inch disks store 1.2M. You can't use a high-density disk in a low-density drive.

The original 3 1/2-inch disk stored 720K; a high-density 3 1/2-inch disk can store 1.4M. You can use either type of disk in a 3 1/2-inch drive.

Check the Box Look on the floppy disk box. If it says DS,DD, it is a low-density disk. If it says DS,HD, it's a high-density disk.

Which Drive Do You Need?

If you are buying your first computer and don't use a computer at work, you can probably get by with one 3 1/2-inch disk drive. These are the most popular size disks because they are sturdier.

If you already have a computer and you have programs and data on 5 1/4-inch disks, get a computer with both. Also, if your office computer uses only 5 1/4-inch disks, you will want to get a computer with both.

CD-ROM Drives

Many computers now include a CD-ROM drive. This type of drive enables you to read information from a CD-ROM disc. CD-ROM discs can store a lot of information. For example, you can get an entire encyclopedia on one CD. Many multimedia programs, such as games and educational software, come on CDs. Also, some programs, such as Microsoft Office, come on a CD. Because CDs are becoming so popular, you will most likely want to consider purchasing a PC with this type of drive. For more information on CD-ROM drives, see Lesson 13.

Other Drives

Advertisements may mention the number of drive bays a computer has. You can use these additional drive bays to add other drives. You definitely need a hard drive and at least one floppy drive. In some cases, you may want to consider additional drives.

Having another drive is especially handy for making backups or extra copies of the data on your hard disk. If something happens to the hard disk or if you accidentally delete something you need, you can use the backup to retrieve the information.

In most cases, you can back up the information to floppy disks. Or if you have two hard disks, you can back up from one hard disk to the other. If you have a lot of data to back up, you may want to get an additional drive for backing up. Here are some options:

- Tape backup. Tape backup drives are fairly inexpensive (around $500), can store lots of information (up to 1 gigabyte on a tape), and work fairly quickly.

- Bernoulli drive. Another option for making backups is a Bernoulli drive. These drives are reliable, removable, use a disk similar to a floppy drive, and can store a lot of information.

- Optical drive. This type of drive uses a laser beam to read and write information. The drives can store a lot of information (hundreds of megabytes) and are portable. You can write, change, and delete data on this type of drive. On the down side, the drive is slower than a hard drive, so you probably wouldn't want to use this type of drive for anything other than mass storage or backup.

Summary Checklist

Use this summary checklist to note the size and type of drive you want. Or you can make a copy of the checklist and then, for comparison, fill in the information for each of the computer systems you are considering.

1. Fill in the size, speed, and type of hard disk you need.

Size: _____

Speed: _____

Type: _____

2. Check the type(s) of drive you want:

❑   5 1/4-inch drive

❑   3 1/2-inch drive

❑   CD-ROM drive

3. Check any other type drive you need:

❑   Additional hard drive

❑   Tape drive

Lesson 8

Other System Unit Considerations

In this lesson, you will learn about expansion slots and ports, power supply, and system unit case styles.

Expansion Slots

When you purchase a computer, you need to plan for the future. What you need today is different from what you will need in two years. As you become more proficient with the computer, you will want to use it to do more things.

Most computers enable you to plan for growth by including expansion slots. These slots are similar to plugs. You can add electronic cards, such as a sound card or fax/modem card, by plugging the card into the slot (see Figure 8.1). These electronic cards may be called expansion cards, cards, boards, or add-on boards. They all mean the same thing.

When you purchase a computer, check the following expansion slot specs:

- **Number of slots.** Make sure that you have enough expansion slots. You probably need a minimum of three to four open slots.

- **Bit width or bus.** Slots, like processors, can move different amounts of data, depending on the number of paths, or bits. For example: 8-bit cards move 8 bits, 16-bit cards move 16 bits, and 32-bit cards move 32 bits. The more bits, the faster the card works. If you want to add a 32-bit expansion card, then you need at least one 32-bit expansion slot. You will want to know the bit size of the expansion slots in the computer.

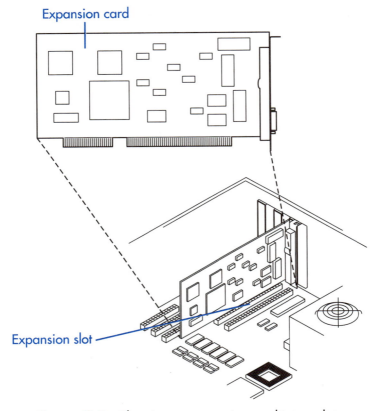

Figure 8.1 Plugging an expansion card into a slot.

- **Bus Architecture.** Like processors, different expansion slots and cards use different bus architecture. ISA (Industry Standard Architecture) cards are 16-bit. EISA (Enhanced Industry Standard Architecture) cards are 32-bit. MCA (MicroChannel

Architecture) are 16- or 32-bit and are only in IBM computers. VESA buses, introduced in 1993, can send and receive data faster because they run at the system's clock speed rather than the bus clock speed. PCI buses provide a 32-bit path between the CPU and peripherals. This type of bus is better in the long run than the VESA because it incorporates features from newer processors. (Lesson 6 covers buses in more detail.)

Remember that expansion cards only work with a specific bus. That means the system and the peripheral must have the same specification or you won't get the added performance. For example, you must have a card designed for a VESA bus and a VESA bus to get all the benefits of the technology.

Ports

On back of the computer, there are little connectors called *ports*. You use these connectors to plug in additional equipment (called *peripherals*), such as a printer, mouse, keyboard, monitor, and so on.

Most computers already have ports for the keyboard, monitor, and sometimes the mouse. In addition, the computer should have other "blank" ports that you can use to hook up equipment you need.

There are two types of ports: serial and parallel. Serial ports send information one bit at a time (serially). You can use this type of port to attach serial printers, a mouse, and modem. Keep in mind that the device you hook up to the port must match the port type. You hook up serial devices to serial ports. Most computers have at least two serial ports (which are referred to as COM1 and COM2).

Parallel ports send information 8 bits at a time over eight wires; most computers have at least one parallel port named LPT1. You can use this type of port to hook up devices designed for parallel ports. For instance, most printers hook up with a parallel port.

Some expansion cards also have ports. You plug the card into the expansion slot *inside* the computer, and part of the card (the port) fits through the back of the computer. You can then use this port.

Power Supply

The system unit also contains a power supply used to power the electronic components. All computers come with a power supply. Be sure it is powerful enough for the equipment you have now as well as for any equipment you plan to add—most PCs sold today have 200-watt power supplies, which is acceptable.

Case Styles

The final system unit consideration is the size or style of the case. The size of the case is the *footprint*. There are three basic styles: tower, desktop, and slimline (see Figure 8.2).

To decide which type of case you need, ask yourself these questions:

- Where will I use the computer? How much room do I have? If you don't have a lot of room on the desk, you may want to get a tower model. The system unit can sit on the floor. A slimline model also doesn't take up much space. (If you intend to use

Other System Unit Considerations

the computer away from home or the office, you should consider a portable computer, discussed in Lesson 16.)

- What will I be adding to the computer? The size of the case can affect the number of available expansion slots. For instance, a slimline model won't have as much room for expansion as a tower model.

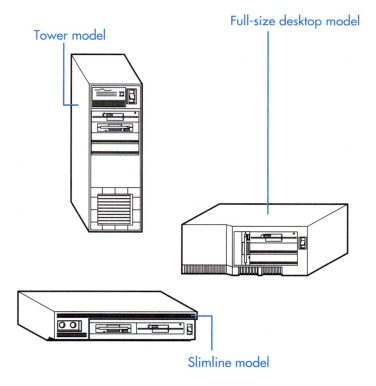

Figure 8.2 Different case styles.

Summary Checklist

You can complete the checklist and write in the system unit specifications you want. Then as you shop for a system, compare your list with the particular system. Or you can make a copy of the checklist and then use it to record the specifications for each system unit you want to shop for.

# of expansion slots   _____

Bit size of slots   _____

Bus architecture   _____

# of ports   _____

Type of ports   _____

Power supply wattage   _____

    Check the case style you want:

        ❑   Tower

        ❑   Desktop

        ❑   Slimline

Lesson 9

Monitors

In this lesson, you will learn about the different types of monitors as well as how to be sure you get a monitor that will meet your needs.

Differences in Monitors

A monitor is a critical component of your computer system: You must have a monitor. Because you will be staring at the monitor every time you use the computer, you want to be sure to get a good monitor.

Monitors differ in these ways:

- Crispness of the image displayed (known as the *resolution*).
- Standard used.
- Size of the monitor.
- Other features that make the monitor work better or more quickly.

> **Be Sure the Monitor Is Included**   Sometimes, advertisements will show a really low price for a computer. When you read the fine print, you will note that it says the monitor is not part of the offer. If you run across any "bargains," make sure the offer includes a monitor or be sure to add the price of the monitor to the system to get a "true" price.

Monitors and Adapters

A monitor is usually two pieces of hardware equipment: the TV-like box that sits on your desk and an electronic adapter card (called a video adapter card or just video card) stored inside the system unit. Sometimes, the video card is a part of the motherboard.

Most of the time, the monitor comes with its own video card, but you can also buy each piece individually. The important part of the duo is the video card; it controls the features and quality of the monitor.

Resolution

The *resolution* is the crispness or sharpness of a monitor. A few things control the resolution:

- The number of pixels displayed. *Pixel* is short for *picture element* and is the smallest unit used to create an image. Computer monitors measure the number of pixels displayed horizontally and vertically, so you will see a resolution of 640 × 480 or 1024 × 768.

- The dot pitch, measured in millimeters (mm). The smaller the number, the better. A good dot pitch is .28mm.

- The refresh rate or the rate the electrons scan the screen. Your computer measures this rate in hertz (Hz). The higher the hertz, the better. In addition to the rate, you may see *multi-scan* or *multi-frequency*. This means that the monitor can adapt to suit any scanning frequency. You may also see a note saying the monitor is *interlaced* (scans only every other line) or *non-interlaced*. Because interlaced monitors can flicker, you will probably want to get a non-interlaced monitor.

Monitors

70 Hz Scan A good scan rate is 70 Hz or more.

When you are looking at ads, you will probably see some (if not all) of this information included. The critical spec is the number of pixels. You want at least 640 × 480 or more. Also, there's no better test than just looking at the monitor yourself. Do some things and watch the monitor. Does it flicker? Does it look crisp? Compare other monitors to see which you prefer.

Monitor Standards

Just like there are standards for buses and other equipment, there are display *standards*. The following table explains each of the display standards:

Name	Description
SVGA or SuperVGA	The newest monitor standard. Same colors as the VGA. Resolution of 1024 × 768 or more. This standard varies from brand to brand.
VGA	Can display 256 colors simultaneously out of a palette of over 200,000 colors. Resolutions range from 640 × 480 to 800 × 600.
EGA (Enhanced Graphics Adapter)	Old standard. Can display 16 colors. Resolution of 640 × 350.

Name	Description
CGA (Color Graphics Adapter)	Old standard. Can display 2 or 4 colors simultaneously. Resolution of 320 × 200 (4 colors) or 640 × 200 (2 colors).
MDA (Monochrome Display Adapter)	Oldest standard. Can display text in 1 color. Cannot display graphics.

SVGA or VGA Is OK! When you buy a monitor, you want either a VGA or a SuperVGA.

Size

Measure your computer monitor the same way you measure your TV: diagonally. Most monitors sold are 15-inch and are suitable for most applications. If you do a lot of desktop publishing or work with graphics quite a bit, you may want to invest in a larger monitor. For example, you can get a 17-inch monitor that can display two pages. Keep in mind that these larger monitors can be expensive.

Other Features

In addition to the resolution, standard, and size, a monitor may include additional features that make it work more quickly or create a better image. In particular, the amount of memory and bus type can affect the speed and quality of a monitor.

Memory

A video card has built-in memory to process the image. The amount of memory a card has affects the complexity of the image it can display, the speed at which it can display things, and the resolution and number of colors it can display. Remember that computers measure memory in kilobytes (K or KB) or megabytes (M or MB) and that more memory is better. At the minimum, look for one with at least 1M.

Bus Type

You will see some monitors advertised as local bus video. Remember that the bus is how the hardware connects. A local bus video uses a special chip to speed up the communication between the microprocessor and the video card. Having a local bus video, then, is a plus.

VESA is another bus type. VESA (Video Electronics Standards Association) is a group of companies that set standards for video cards and monitors. VESA buses provide better performance than ISA buses. PCI (Peripheral Component Interconnect) is the latest bus type. For more information on buses, see Lesson 6.

Video Accelerators

Another way to speed up processing images is to use a video accelerator card. If you do a lot of intense work on graphics, you may want to purchase this type of video card. Keep in mind that it's hard to predict how a particular card will work on a particular system. You may not gain any speed.

Knobs and Swivels

There are a couple of little knobs and swivels on monitors that you can use to adjust its settings. To adjust the brightness and contrast, you will probably have two knobs on the front, side, or back of the monitor. The monitor also has its own power switch.

The Computer Doesn't Work! If you turn on the computer and nothing happens, make sure that you also turn on the monitor and check the brightness and contrast. People often make this mistake.

The monitor should also come on a stand that swivels so that you can adjust it. Sometimes, it comes on a plain stand that doesn't allow you to tilt or turn your monitor. Or it doesn't come on a stand at all. If that's the case, ask the salesperson you're buying the computer from to throw in a monitor stand.

Summary Checklist

When you are shopping for a monitor, use this checklist. You can complete the checklist with the type of monitor you want and then compare the list to monitors you find. Or you can make copies of the checklist and use them to record the specifications for each monitor you check out.

1. Check the type of monitor.

❑ SuperVGA

❑ VGA

2. What's the resolution?

_____

3. What's the dot pitch?

_____

4. What's the size?

_____

Monitors

5. Amount of memory?

_____

6. Check any that apply:

❑   Non-interlaced

❑   Local bus video

Lesson

Keyboard and Mouse

In this lesson, you will learn about the different types of input devices: the keyboard, mouse, and others.

Keyboards

All computers consist of at least three pieces of hardware: the monitor, system unit, and keyboard. Keyboards come with most computers, and they all work they same way. You press the key just like you press a key on a typewriter.

Keyboards have different keys than a typewriter, though. Figure 10.1 shows the most common type of keyboard layout, the Enhanced Layout.

Figure 10.1 The Enhanced Keyboard.

Keyboard Keys

In addition to the letter and number keys, keyboards also include special keys:

- **Function keys.** Function keys are F1 through F12 and perform different functions depending on the program. For instance, pressing F1 in many Windows-based programs displays help information.

Keyboard and Mouse

The most common keyboards have function keys both along the left and the top of the keyboard. Why? Original keyboards had the function keys along the left. Then companies developed a newer keyboard with the function keys along the top. If you were used to the function keys along the left, it was hard to get used to the keys at the top. So now most keyboards accommodate both (left and top).

- **Numeric keypad.** Most keyboards have a separate numeric keypad to the far right of the keyboard. When you press the Num Lock key, you can use this keypad to enter numbers. When the Num Lock key is off, pressing these keys moves the cursor around on-screen.

- **Editing and cursor movement keys.** In addition to the cursor movement keys on the numeric keypad, a keyboard may have an additional set of editing and cursor movement keys next to the numeric keypad.

- **Program keys.** Some keyboards include a row of program keys to the right of the function keys. These keys usually include Print Screen, Scroll Lock, and Break. If you can program your keyboard, you will also have keys for programming and remapping the keyboard (changing which key does what).

Be Careful of Programmable Keys!
If you can program your keyboard (change the function of the keys), be careful. It's easy to touch the program or remap key when you didn't mean to. Then you may end up pressing F and getting T. Check your computer documentation if you accidentally remap or program a key.

What to Look for in Keyboards

You may think that as long as the keyboard has the right keys, you will be fine. But when you are buying a computer, you should check the following:

- The touch of the keyboard. Different keyboards feel differently when you type on them. Some are stiff and may clack when you type. Some are squishy. Try out the keyboard to be sure you like the feel of it. It really does make a difference!

- The layout. Be sure the layout of the keys is comfortable for you, especially if you are used to another computer and want a similar layout.

- Consider getting accessories that make the keyboard more comfortable, such as wrist rests. When you do the same thing over and over with your wrists and fingers, you can develop RSI, or repetitive stress injury, such as carpal tunnel syndrome. To protect against this, you should position the keyboard so that when you type, your fingers are even with your wrists (not bent way up or bent way down). Your hands should be parallel to the floor.

- To prevent wrist injuries, new keyboards have been designed that support the wrist. You may want to purchase a PC with this type of keyboard or inquire about buying this type of keyboard separately.

Mice

Many new computers come bundled today with a *mouse*. A mouse is a hand-held device the shape and size of a bar of soap (see Figure 10.2). You slide the mouse around on the desktop and the on-screen mouse pointer moves accordingly. You can use a mouse in many programs, especially Microsoft Windows programs, to select commands, start programs, draw, and so on. Some programs *require* a mouse.

Most programs let you use either a mouse or a keyboard, but some functions (such as drawing) may be available only with a mouse.

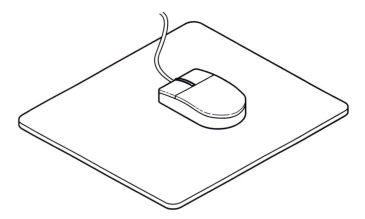

Figure 10.2 A mouse.

How Mice Differ

Mice differ in these ways:

- **Type of mouse.** A serial mouse connects to a PC's serial port. (Lesson 8 discusses ports in more detail.) A bus mouse comes with an expansion card that you plug into an empty expansion slot inside your computer. The bus connects to the card. Some computers come with a "mouse" port. You can hook up a bus mouse to this port.

  > **Your Call** If you don't want to use one of your serial ports for your mouse, get a bus mouse.

- **Manufacturer of mouse.** Different companies manufacture mice. The most popular is the Microsoft mouse.

- **Number of buttons.** Some mice have two buttons, some have three. If a program can use a mouse, it usually relies on the left mouse button. Sometimes, you can use the right mouse button to activate shortcuts—it depends on the program. Very few programs take advantage of the third button on three-button mice.

- **Software.** The mouse needs a special program, called a *driver* to tell the computer and other programs how the mouse works. The program usually comes with the mouse.

- **Look and feel.** Different mice feel differently. You should try out the mouse and make sure that it is comfortable.

You will also want to get a mouse pad to put on your desk. You slide the mouse on the mouse pad, which gives you better control of the mouse's movement. Mouse pads are very inexpensive. There are many companies that distribute promotional mouse pads; ask your salesperson for one. If you have to pay for a mouse pad, it should only cost about a buck.

Other Input Devices

In addition to the keyboard and mouse, you may want to consider other input devices, depending on your needs.

Trackballs

A *trackball* is like an upside-down mouse with the roller ball exposed. To make a movement, you roll the ball itself. Many portable computers use a trackball (see Lesson 16 for more on portable computers). Also, if you don't have a lot of room on your desk, you may want to get a trackball.

Joysticks

If you want to play games with your computer, you need to invest in a *joystick*. A joystick is similar to an arcade control. You can move the hand-held stick to the left, right, back, or forward and it has buttons. You can use a joystick, for example, to shoot at invaders or to maneuver a plane.

Scanners

If you work extensively with graphic images, you may want to purchase a *scanner*. A scanner converts a printed image into an electronic image that you can manipulate on the computer. For example, you can scan in a photograph of your dog. You can purchase a flat-bed scanner that works like a photocopier; a sheet-fed scanner that works by feeding through the image you want to scan; or a hand-held scanner that works by moving the scanner over the image.

If you have a lot of printed material, such as contracts or catalog information, you can use a scanner to scan in text. In addition to the scanner, you will need OCR (optical character recognition) software to translate the image into text. You need to check out the scanner and software carefully to make sure it will suit your purpose. OCR software varies wildly in how accurate and fast it works.

In this lesson, you learned about keyboards, mice, and other input devices. In the next lesson, you'll learn about printers.

Lesson 11

Printers

In this lesson, you will learn the types of printers that are available and how to select a printer that is appropriate for your needs.

Why Buy a Printer?

When you purchase a computer, you will also most likely want to purchase a printer. A printer enables you to print the information you create on the computer: reports, memos, graphs, budgets, and so on.

Printers range in price from $150 for a relatively slow dot-matrix printer to several thousand dollars for a high-quality color laser printer. To select a printer, you need to assess what you want to print, the quality you need, and the price you want to pay. These factors will help you determine the best printer for your situation.

It Never Hurts to Ask! When you are shopping for a computer, ask the salesperson if you can get a price break if you also purchase the printer at the same time. Some salespeople will give you a deal if you buy both items together.

Types of Printers

All printers connect to a computer in the same way: with a cable. When you issue a command to print, the computer sends the information over the cable to the printer. The printer, like a computer, then processes the information and creates the printed page.

Printers differ in the way they create the page, the quality of the printed page, and the speed with which they create the page. There are three basic types of printers, and each has a unique print method, quality, and speed:

- Dot-matrix printers
- Inkjet printers
- Laser printers

You can also purchase color printers. You probably don't need one if you just want to print out letters or forms. However, if you do a lot of presentations, you may want to look into color printers.

Dot-Matrix Printers

Dot-matrix printers are the most popular type of printers. On the plus side, they are cheap, reliable, and have minimal operating cost. On the down side, these printers are noisy and slow, don't print graphics well, and have limited typefaces.

The following checklist summarizes some instances where you might consider using a dot-matrix printer:

- Quality is not a big concern; you just want a cheap, reliable printer.

- You need to print multipart forms. Dot-matrix printers are the only types of printers you can use to print multipart forms.

- You need to print on wide paper (11-by-17-inch), and print quality is not important (for example, wide reports or banners).

- You have access to a better printer, and you need the dot-matrix only to print draft versions of documents.

How a Dot-Matrix Printer Works

The printhead on the dot-matrix printer contains a series of tiny pins, either 9 or 24 pins. The printer works by firing this series of pins. When the printer fires a pin, it strikes the ribbon and places a dot on the page. The combination of dots forms patterns to make characters and graphics. If you've ever looked closely at a printout from a dot-matrix printer, you may see these little dots.

Critical Purchase Decisions

If you decide to purchase a dot-matrix printer, here are the critical things to consider:

- **Cost.** Dot-matrix printers range in price from $150 up. The more expensive the printer, the better the quality and the faster the speed.

- **Quality.** The quality, or resolution, depends on the number of pins in the print head (9 or 24). The more pins, the better the quality. The resolution is measured in dots per inch (dpi). The typical resolution is 360 dpi for a 24-pin printer. The printer will also be rated by the number of columns it can print.

- **Speed.** Measured by how many characters per second (cps) the printer can print. Most dot-matrix printers can print in two speeds: draft and near-letter quality (NLQ). Draft speeds range from 240 cps to over 400 cps (about three lines per second). NLQ speeds range from 48 cps to 130+ cps.

- **Paper handling.** Some printers use a single-sheet feed, that is, the printer carrier holds single sheets of paper and feeds them through the printer. Others use a push/pull tractor. With this type of feed, the paper has little holes along the edges that feed through the printer, around the roller bar, and between the ribbon and roller bar. Sometimes, it is troublesome to get the paper to feed correctly.

- **Fonts.** A dot-matrix printer uses a limited number of fonts: usually 12 to 14 fonts. You can also use TrueType fonts.

TrueType Printer language included with Microsoft Windows. Rather than rely on the fonts included with the printer, your hard disk stores TrueType fonts in files. When you print with these fonts, the software program sends the instructions on creating the font to the printer.

How You Count Your Fonts Before you buy a printer, ask to see a printout of all the fonts it can print. Don't be mislead by the advertised number of printer fonts because the manufacturer counts each *style* of a typeface as a font. For example, the manufacturer may count Times Roman, Times Italic, and Times Bold as three different fonts, when actually they are three different styles of the same font (Times).

Inkjet Printers

Inkjet printers are midrange printers; that is, they are in between the dot-matrix printers and laser printers in terms of cost and quality. (The next section discusses the laser printer.) On the plus side, the price and quality are usually reasonable, and they are quiet. On the down side, the speed is slow, and the cost to operate is high. When you run out of ink, you usually have to replace both the ink cartridge and the print head. Also, sometimes the ink can run or smudge on the paper.

The following checklist summarizes some instances where you might consider using an inkjet printer:

- You want quality output, but can't afford a laser printer.
- Speed is not important.
- You want a printer you can take with you on the road. Some manufacturers offer portable versions of inkjet printers.
- You want to be able to print in color. If you want a quality color printer, the most affordable color printers are color inkjet printers.

How an Inkjet Printer Works

This type of printer uses an ink-filled cartridge and a tiny nozzle to spray ink onto the page in a series of dots. These tiny, precise dots make the characters and graphics.

Critical Purchase Decisions

If you decide to purchase an inkjet printer, here are the critical things to consider:

- **Cost.** Range in price from $300 up.
- **Quality.** Dots per inch (dpi) determine the resolution (usually 300 to 360 dpi).
- **Speed.** How many pages per minute (ppm) the printer can print. The average speed is 2 ppm, compared to 4 and up for laser printers.
- **Fonts.** The number of fonts will vary. You can use TrueType fonts.

Laser Printers

Laser printers offer top-of-the line quality and speed, and are fairly affordable. If you do a lot of printing and want the best quality, consider this type of printer.

How a Laser Printer Works

A laser printer works like a copy machine. Inside the printer, chemicals cover a drum. When you print, a laser beam magnetizes the particles on the drum, creating the image of the page on the drum. These particles attract a fine powdered ink, called *toner*. As the paper moves through the printer, the pressure and heat of the printer presses the toner off the drum and onto the page.

Critical Purchase Decisions

If you decide to purchase a laser printer, here are the critical things to consider:

- **Cost.** Range in price from $650 up. You will need to replace the toner cartridge periodically; cartridges cost $60 or more.

- **Quality.** Dots per inch (dpi) determine the resolution. Resolution can range from 300 dpi up to 1,000 dpi. The higher the resolution, the more expensive the printer.

- **Speed.** How many pages per minute (ppm) the printer can print. The average speed ranges from 4 ppm to 8 ppm.

- **Fonts.** Most laser printers come with several fonts. You can also usually add additional fonts using cartridges, and you can use TrueType fonts.

- **Memory.** Because this type of printer creates an image of the entire page, it requires memory to store the image. The printer also needs memory to

Lesson 11

store the fonts used on the page. Most printers come with some memory, and you can usually add more memory later.

More Is Better Remember that you always want as much memory as possible; this applies not only to the computer system, but also to your printer.

- **Language.** Laser printers "talk" in different languages. The most common printer languages are PCL (developed by Hewlett-Packard) and PostScript. PostScript printers provide more typefaces and are more expensive.

Summary Checklist

Use this summary checklist to decide what type of printer you need:

1. Check the type of documents you will most likely print. Then read the type of printer most appropriate for that type of output.

What will you mostly print?	Type of printer you can use
❑ Correspondence (letters, memos)	Any
❑ Published materials (newsletters, reports, manuscripts)	Laser
❑ Graphics (charts, drawings, clip art)	Inkjet or laser

❑	Forms	Dot-matrix
❑	Database reports on wide paper	Dot-matrix
❑	Color presentations	Color inkjet

2. Check the most important factor to you in selecting a printer. This answer will help you determine how much emphasis to give the answers to the next three questions.

- ❑ Quality
- ❑ Price
- ❑ Speed

3. How important is quality? Consider the type of printer next to the box you check:

Suggested Printer Type

❑	Not important	Dot-matrix
❑	Fairly important	Inkjet
❑	Very important	Laser

4. How important is price? Consider the type of printer next to the box you check:

Suggested Printer Type

❑	Not important	Laser
❑	Fairly important	Inkjet
❑	Very important	Dot-matrix

5. How important is speed? Consider the type of printer next to the box you check:

                              Suggested Printer Type

- ❏ Not important   Inkjet
- ❏ Fairly important   Dot-matrix
- ❏ Very important   Laser

Lesson 12

Communications

In this lesson, you learn the ways you can use your computer to communicate as well as the equipment you need if you want to take advantage of this capability.

Understanding Communications

Using your computer to communicate with other computers can connect you to the "global village." You can send and receive data from your desktop PC to a computer that's thousands of miles away. Being able to hook up with other computers gives you access not only to other computer users but to a wealth of information. The next section gives some examples of what you can do.

What You Can Do

Using your PC and the appropriate communication equipment, you can do the following:

- **Dial another computer directly to transmit files.** For example, using your modem, you can call up your work PC from home and copy a file from your home PC to your work PC or vice versa. As another example, suppose that you are in New York and need to send a proposal to someone in California. Using the communication equipment, you can do so in a matter of minutes.

- **Connect with a bulletin board system (BBS).** A bulletin board system is a computer system usually set up and run by an individual, and usually dedicated to a purpose or hobby. For example, you may find a BBS in your area devoted to mysteries. You can call up the BBS to chat with other BBS subscribers, download (copy from the BBS to your computer) files, and review BBS information.

- **Connect with an on-line service.** An on-line service is a sophisticated BBS run by professionals for profit. Using this type of service, you can read about current news events, shop, send electronic mail to other computer users hooked up to the service, review current stock prices, and more. Popular on-line services include Prodigy, America Online, and CompuServe.

- **Connect to the Internet.** The Internet is basically a loosely connected network of networks. Not one person or company owns the Internet. It's like thousands and thousands of BBSs and on-line services linked together. You can get access to the Internet through some of the commercial on-line services. Or you can contact an Internet provider to get connected.

- **Send a fax from your computer to another computer or fax machine.** As discussed in the "Buying a Fax Modem" section later in this lesson, you can purchase a modem that also functions as a fax machine. You can create documents on your PC and then fax them to another PC or to a fax machine. You can also receive faxes from other PCs or fax machines.

What You Need

To take advantage of the communication features of your computer, you need the following three items:

- A modem
- Communication software

- A telephone line

The next sections describe each of these required items in more detail.

Buying a Modem

To use your PC to communicate with other PCs, you first need a modem. When you shop for a computer system, take a look at some of the system bundles. Sometimes, a bundle will include a modem as part of the package. Or you can buy the modem separately—when you purchase the computer system or at a later time.

How a Modem Works

The computer uses digital information (0s and 1s). A phone line, on the other hand, transmits information using analog signals (sound waves). That's where the modem comes in. Modem stands for MOdulator-DEModulator, which means it translates the digital information to analog and sends the analog information over the phone lines. The receiving modem then translates the analog information back to digital.

In the future, all phone lines will be fiber-optic cables and will be able to transmit digital signals directly. This means that you won't need a modem.

Speed

One of the most important factors in selecting a modem is the modem speed. When you use the telephone line or hook up to an on-line service, the on-line service charges you for the connect time. The shorter the time, the less expensive the charge. Therefore, you want a modem that can connect and transmit data quickly.

Modem speed is measured in baud rate and ranges from 2400 to 28800 (28.8). Purchase at least a 14.4 to 28.8 baud modem. The terms *baud* and *bits per second* (bps) are often used interchangeably. They're different; baud refers to the modem's capabilities and bps refers to the total data throughput, including any compression.

Keep in mind that your modem can work only as fast as the connecting modem. So if you have a 19200 bps modem and you call a 2400 bps modem, you can send information only at the 2400 bps speed.

> **Compression Features Save Time**
> Some modems also come with data compression technology. Using this feature, the modem squeezes, or compresses, the files so that they are smaller. Because the files are smaller, they won't take as much time to transmit.

Internal or External

In addition to speed, you will also need to decide whether you want an internal or external modem. An internal modem is an electronic board that you install inside the system unit (see Figure 12.1). This type of modem may be cheaper than an external because you don't have the case or lights. If you have a lot of free expansion slots, you may want to select this type of modem. (See Lesson 8 for more information on expansion slots.)

If you are short on expansion slots, you may want to get an external modem. An external modem sits outside the system unit and connects to your computer by a cable. This type of modem enables you to visually check the progress of a transmission by watching the lights. Also, this modem may be easier to install than an internal modem. On the down side, this modem may be more expensive, and you will have to use one of your serial ports to connect the modem. (Lesson 8 explains ports in detail.)

Communications

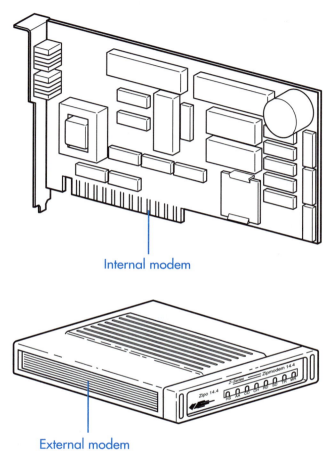

Figure 12.1 An internal and external modem.

Buying a Fax Modem

In addition to a standard modem than can send and receive information, you can also purchase a special type of modem called a *fax modem*. Using your computer and a fax modem, you can send and receive faxes over the phone line.

A regular fax machine works like a photocopy machine. You feed the paper through that you want to send. The fax machine translates this image and then sends the image over the phone lines. The receiving fax machine translates and prints the image.

A fax modem does the same thing only you don't feed the paper through. Instead, you create the document you want to fax on the computer. Then using the fax modem, you can send this document over the phone lines to any type of fax machine (not just computer fax modems). Keep in mind that you can't fax paper copies using a fax modem; you can send only documents created using the computer.

Your computer can also receive faxes. You can view them on-screen or have them printed directly to your printer.

Fax modems differ in these ways:

- **Speed.** Bits per second (bps) determine the fax modem speed, like a regular modem. The higher the number, the faster the transmission.

- **Send/Receive features.** Some fax modems can only send faxes. You want to be sure the fax modem can both send and receive.

- **Software.** Just as you need software to use a regular modem, you need software to handle the fax. Some fax modems come bundled with software. Or you can purchase a fax software program. The most popular is WinFax Pro.

Selecting Software

In addition to a modem, you also need a software program to manage the communication between the modem and the computer. Some modems come bundled with software. This software usually includes the bare minimum of features. If your needs are simple, this software may be all you need.

Communications

Attention! Windows 95 comes with a simple communications program called HyperTerminal. You may be able to use this program.

If your needs are more complex, you may want to purchase a full-featured communication program. ProComm Plus, for example, is a popular communication program. In this case, be sure to plan for the added expense of the software.

Hooking Up a Telephone Line

The final piece of the communication package is a telephone line, which you connect to the modem. If you don't want to use your regular phone line, you can call the phone company and have them install an additional line. You will then have a separate, dedicated phone line and phone number for your modem.

If you don't want the added expense of two phone lines, you can use your existing phone line. When you use the same line, you have to coordinate the use of the line. That is, if someone wants to send you a file or fax, they will need to call you first so that you can set up the phone line to receive the call.

Once you have the modem, communication software, and phone line, you can dial up the world!

Summary Checklist

Use this checklist to summarize your modem needs.

1. Check the type of modem you want:

❑   Modem

  ❑   Internal

  ❑   External

Lesson 12

- Fax modem
    - Internal
    - External

2. Check the speed:
- 14400 (14.4) bps
- 28800 (28.8) bps
- Other_____

3. Check any other feature included:
- Includes communication software

    Software type:_____
- Includes data compression

Lesson 13

Multimedia PCs

In this lesson, you will learn what makes up a multimedia PC as well as whether you should purchase this type of PC.

What Is Multimedia?

Multimedia is one of the newest buzz words in computing. It is the combination of information in different formats (text, audio, graphics). When you purchase a multimedia PC, you can both create and play back multimedia information.

What's a Multimedia PC?

A multimedia PC, or *MPC*, is a PC with at least the following equipment:

- CD-ROM drive used for accessing and storing multimedia information.
- Sound card and speakers used for playing back the audio information. If you want to record information, you also need a microphone.

In addition, a multimedia PC may also include a joystick (see Lesson 10). The "Buying a Multimedia PC" section discusses some of the other specs for this type of computer. For now, you just need to understand what makes a PC capable of performing multimedia tasks.

What You Can Do with Multimedia

With your multimedia PC, you can run multimedia applications. Most of the multimedia applications available today are for educational or recreational purposes. For instance, you can get the entire Encyclopedia Brittanica on disk. The multimedia encyclopedia not only includes the "flat" text and pictures you might expect in a printed encyclopedia, but a multimedia encyclopedia also includes sounds and graphics. You can hear the sound a hummingbird makes or see a giraffe gallop across the plains.

You can also buy almanacs, dictionaries, atlases, books of quotations, histories, and literature collections on CD-ROM. You can purchase musical collections, such as the complete works of Mozart, for your computer.

Because you can store a lot of information on a CD-ROM, you can purchase disks packed full of software or clip art. Some popular application programs come in CD-ROM versions.

You can also use your multimedia PC to create multimedia applications. For example, using the PC and special software, you can create sophisticated presentations that, for example, explain the manufacturing process used to create a product. This presentation may show an animated sequence of the process, as well as a video clip of the product designer. The product designer can explain how the process works.

Do You Need a Multimedia PC?

Now that you know what is possible, you may wonder whether you need a multimedia PC. There are two basic reasons for buying this type of computer. The first is that you are a sophisticated user and want to create multimedia applications. In this case, you should check the requirements of the software you want to use and be sure to get the necessary equipment to run the software.

The second reason you may want to buy a multimedia PC is that you have children. Because most of the multimedia software available is recreational or educational, your children will benefit most from a multimedia PC. Many games and educational software require a sound card or a CD-ROM drive.

Understanding the MPC Logo

The Multimedia PC Marketing Council set these original standards for multimedia PCs, and they are as follows:

386SX-based PC or higher

Minimum 16MHz clock speed

2MB of RAM

30MB hard drive

1.44MB 3.5-inch floppy drive

101-key keyboard

serial port

parallel port

VGA card and monitor with 640 × 480 resolution at 256 colors

2-button mouse

joystick

MIDI port

MPC-compatible sound card

MPC-compatible CD-ROM drive

If a computer meets the standard, the manufacturer can use the official MPC logo. You may think looking for this logo is all you need to do when purchasing a multimedia PC. It's not. You need to keep in mind a few cautions.

First, the MPC standard is a measure of what the computer has; not how good it is. You can't select a multimedia PC based on the logo only. You must look closely at the standards of the system.

Second, the standards are the *minimum* system requirements. If you review the requirement list, you can easily see that the machine isn't very powerful. You will probably want a system that exceeds these minimum standards.

Third, the standards are periodically updated, so you may see an MPC logo on a computer that met the first set of standards, but aren't up to spec for the newest standards.

The bottom line is that when you purchase a multimedia PC, you need to take a close look at what the system has and what you need. The next section discusses strategies for buying a multimedia PC.

Buying a Multimedia PC

If you decide you need a multimedia PC, you can purchase this type of computer using one of the following strategies:

- You can purchase a multimedia PC as a complete package. The package should include, at the minimum, a high-powered system (at least a Pentium with 16MB RAM and 800MB hard disk), a sound card, speakers, and a CD-ROM drive.

- You can purchase a "regular" PC and then additionally purchase a sound card, speakers, and CD-ROM drive. You can purchase the additional components individually or as a "multimedia kit." Be sure the "regular" PC meets or exceeds the requirements mentioned in the preceding paragraph.

- You can purchase just the components you need. For instance, if you just want sound capabilities, you can just purchase a sound card and speakers. If you want a CD-ROM drive, you can purchase that component.

The next two sections describe what to look for when purchasing a sound card and CD-ROM drive.

Buying a Sound Card

If you want to purchase a sound card and speakers, you need to know how these components differ and what to look for. If your PC package includes these components, you will also want to check to be sure the sound card and speakers you are getting are a good value.

A sound card is an electronic card that you insert in an expansion slot inside your PC. The sound card, like all electronic cards, is rated by its bus width. For instance, you can purchase an 8-bit, 16-bit, or 32-bit sound card. The 32-bit card provides better quality sound.

For the software to take advantage of the sound card, it must recognize the card. The most popular sound card is the SoundBlaster card. If you are purchasing a brand other than SoundBlaster, be sure to check the application requirements of the software program. The program should recognize the brand you are buying, or the sound card itself should be SoundBlaster-compatible.

In addition to the sound card, you also need speakers. Sometimes, the speakers are included with the sound card. If not, you need to purchase the speakers separately.

Sound cards range in price from $100 to $300. You can buy speakers for as cheap as $20. If you want stereo-quality speakers, you should plan to pay around $350 to $400.

Buying a CD-ROM Drive

Another component of a multimedia PC is the CD-ROM drive. This drive, similar to a big floppy drive, enables you to read information from a CD-ROM. You can buy, as mentioned, the complete works of Shakespeare on CD-ROM or reference works, such as a dictionary.

A CD-ROM differs from a floppy disk in a few ways. First, you can store an enormous amount of data on a CD-ROM (around 700 MB). You will need this storage capacity because graphics and sound files are huge. Second, you can only read information from—not write information to—a CD-ROM. Hence, the name ROM, or read-only memory.

You can purchase an internal or external CD-ROM drive. If you purchase a CD-ROM drive separately or receive it as part of your entire system, be sure to check the following:

- **Access time.** The access time tells you how fast the drive can find the data you want. A good access time is in the range of 300 milliseconds.

- **Transfer time.** The transfer time tells you how fast the drive can transfer the information to the PC—once it finds the information. A good transfer time is in the 350+ kilobytes per second range.

- **Compatibility.** If you are purchasing your CD-ROM drive and your sound card separately, make sure that they can work together.

- **Included CD-ROM.** Some CD-ROM drives come packaged with CD-ROM titles.

Double-Spin? Triple-Spin? In some advertisements, you may see the terms double-spin or 2X, triple-spin, 3X or quad 4X used. These terms mean the drive is twice (double), three times (triple) or four times (quad) as fast as normal. Be sure to check the access and transfer times because there is no set standard for "normal."

CD-ROM drives range in price from $300 to $1,000.

Summary Checklist

Use this summary checklist to record the multimedia equipment you want to purchase. For questions 2 and 3, you can record the minimum requirements you want and then use this to check the items you are considering. Or you can copy the checklist and then fill in the questions for the equipment you review.

1. Check the following equipment you want:

    ❑ Sound card

    ❑ CD-ROM drive

2. Complete the following information about the sound card:

    Size

    ❑ 8-bit

    ❑ 16-bit

    ❑ 32-bit

    Speakers included?

    ❑ Yes

    ❑ No

3. Complete the following information about the CD-ROM drive:

    Type

    ❑ Internal

    ❑ External

    Access time   _____ milliseconds

    Data transfer rate   _____ kilobytes per second

Lesson 14

Other Equipment

In this lesson, you will learn about other equipment you may need to purchase in addition to the computer system and software.

Furniture

When you buy your new computer, you are going to need a place to put it. And in finding a place to put it, you may need to purchase new office furniture. Here are some items you may want to include in your shopping budget:

- **A desk.** You will need a desk, or other flat surface, on which to place the PC. If you already have a desk, be sure that you can use the computer comfortably. For instance, is the monitor at the right height (eye-level)? Can you type comfortably (with your wrists straight, palms parallel to the floor, elbows at a right angle)? If not, you may want to purchase a desk designed specifically for a computer. These types of desks may include an area for the system unit and a slide-out drawer or ledge for the keyboard.

- **A printer stand.** In addition to the computer, you need a place to put your printer. The printer must be close enough to the computer to connect with a cable. You may be able to purchase a computer desk with an area designed specifically for the printer. Or you can purchase a separate printer stand.

- **A chair.** If you are going to be using your computer for any length of time, you need a comfortable chair.

Supplies

In addition to furniture, you will also need to purchase some supplies for your computer. At the minimum, you will need the following:

- **Disks.** To make extra copies of your data, you need to purchase disks for the floppy drive. Disks range in price from $5.49 for a box of 10 double-density disks to $9.99 for a box of 10 preformatted high-density disks.

- **Printer paper.** To use your printer, you will need to purchase paper for it. Depending on the type, quality, and quantity of paper, the price for paper will vary.

- **Mouse pad.** So that your mouse doesn't get scuffed up sliding on a bare desk, it's a good idea to purchase a mouse pad. This pad saves your mouse from wear and tear and makes it easier to use. Mouse pads are cheap; you can usually find one for about a dollar. There are many companies who give mouse pads away as promotional tools; ask your salesperson if he has any.

- **Power strip.** To make it convenient to plug in and turn on all the equipment (monitor, system unit, printer), you should purchase a power strip. Get one that offers some surge protection, and if power surges really worry you, get a surge suppressor, also known as a surge protector.

- **A surge protector**. A power surge is a spike in electrical current, for example, during an electrical storm. Protecting against power surges is important because a power surge can destroy data on your computer. For utmost protection, you may want to invest in a surge suppressor. (They cost around $50.)

In addition, you may want to purchase additional supplies. These products range from useful to frivolous. Depending on what you do and what you like, you may want to consider the following supplies:

- **Disk holders.** If you will be using a lot of disks, you may want to purchase a disk holder. This holder can help you keep your disks organized.

- **Computer books.** There are general purpose books on how to use a computer as well as books written for specific application programs, such as Microsoft Word for Windows and Microsoft Excel. Que publishes many books especially written for beginning computer users.

- **Text holder or clip.** If you type from hard copy, you can purchase a stand or a clip to hold the text in place vertically, making it easier to read as you type.

- **Cleaning supplies.** You can purchase a disk cleaner, a vacuum to clean out your system unit and keyboard, and other cleaning supplies. If you know what you are doing, consider purchasing and using this equipment. Otherwise, you will probably want to have a service technician handle any cleaning you need done.

- **Wrist rests.** If wrist injuries from repetitive stress injuries (RSI) are a concern, you can purchase wrist rests.

- **Propeller hats.** No comment!

Summary Checklist

Use this checklist to remind yourself of other equipment you need to purchase.

1. Check any additional equipment you need. If you want to be sure to include the price of these items in the budget, write the price of the item next to it.

	Item	**Price**
❏	Desk	_____
❏	Printer stand	_____
❏	Chair	_____
❏	Disks	_____
❏	Printer Paper	_____
❏	Mouse pad	_____
❏	Power supply	_____
❏	Other_____	_____

Lesson 15

Buying a Macintosh

In this lesson, you will learn about the different types of Macintosh computers. If you are thinking of purchasing a Macintosh, review this chapter for pertinent information.

Macintosh Hardware

Macintosh is a type of personal computer manufactured and sold by Apple Computer, Inc. This type of personal computer consists of the same pieces and parts as a PC or IBM computer; a Mac has a system unit, monitor, keyboard, and mouse. This section discusses the similarities and differences between the hardware.

Microprocessor and Memory

As you read in Lesson 6, Intel manufactures microprocessor chips for PCs. Intel numbers the chips 80386, 80486, and so on, and rates their speed in megahertz.

Mac computers also use a microprocessor, but a different company (Motorola) manufactures them and numbers them differently. Most Macs sold have a 68030 microprocessor (equivalent to an 80386) or a 68040 microprocessor (equivalent to an 80486). Speeds range from 50MHz to 132MHz.

Mac computers also use memory to store program instructions and data. Macs measure memory in megabytes. The Mac will have a different amount of memory, depending on the model you select. You can also add memory, usually by plugging in Single Inline Memory Modules (SIMMS) or memory chips into expansion slots. If you purchase a Macintosh, you want as much memory as you can afford.

Disk Drives

To store programs and data, all Mac models come with a hard disk. The hard disk, measured in megabytes, varies from model to model. You should select the largest hard disk you can afford. You can also add another hard drive, if needed.

Most Macs have only one floppy disk drive: a 1.44MB drive called a SuperDrive. On the Mac, you use 3 1/2-inch disks (the same type of disk you can use on a PC). The difference is in the *formatting*. Formatting is the process of preparing the disk for use. You cannot use a disk formatted for the PC on the Mac without reformatting the disk or without using special software.

Some models include a CD-ROM drive as part of the package. If your purchase does not include the drive, you can also buy and add the drive separately.

Monitor

All Mac computers come with an Apple-manufactured monitor. The industry judges Mac monitors by the same factors as a PC monitor: size, resolution, dot-pitch, memory, and so on (see Lesson 9). The most common monitor size is 15-inch. Also, most monitors have a resolution of 640 × 480 and some VRAM, or video RAM.

If you don't like the Macintosh monitor that comes with the model you purchase, you can buy another monitor (bigger size, better resolution) from Apple or from a third-party vendor.

Keyboard and Mouse

All Macs include a keyboard. A Mac keyboard has letter and number keys, like a PC keyboard. However, a Mac keyboard uses different keys, for example, an Option key and a ⌘ (Command) key. A PC keyboard has function keys, but most Mac keyboards do not. If you don't like the keyboard provided with the Mac, you can purchase a different style. There are companies other than Apple that create Mac keyboards.

The mouse is a standard piece of hardware on the Mac. All models include a mouse (made by Apple), and the system unit has a special port for the mouse.

Other Features

All Mac computers include built-in sound capabilities. If you want to play back sounds, you don't have to purchase an additional sound card. If you want to record sound, you may need to purchase a microphone, although some Mac models come with a microphone (see Figure 15.1).

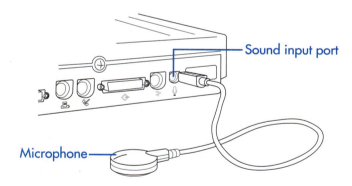

Figure 15.1 The Mac's microphone plugs into a port in the back.

Mac computers include some expansion slots so you can add capabilities, such as a modem. The number will vary. Also so that you can hook up extra equipment, such as a printer, all Mac computers have extra ports. You'll always have a port for the keyboard and mouse. You'll also usually have additional serial and SCSI ports. SCSI stands for Small Computer Systems Interface. You can use this type of port to hook up other devices (scanners, printers, or hard disks). You can also chain together devices using a SCSI interface (sometimes called a *daisy chain*).

Macintosh Software

The Mac uses an operating system known as System. The most current version of System is 7.5 and is in all new Mac models.

In addition to operating system software, some Macs come bundled with software. For example, you may get ClarisWorks as part of the package. You can also purchase software separately. Most popular programs come in both PC and Macintosh versions. If there's something you want to do on the Mac, there's probably software to do it.

Macintosh Lines

If you want to purchase a PC (IBM or compatible), you can purchase the hardware from one of several manufacturers. You can also mix and match the components. For example, you can buy a monitor from one company, a keyboard from another, and a system unit from a third. Because PCs use an open architecture (the design is available to others), other companies can easily manufacture the equipment. If you decide to purchase a PC, you must decide both on the type of PC you want as well as the brand.

Until recently, Macintosh computers had a closed architecture, which meant only Apple knew the design of the hardware and only Apple sold Macintoshes. This has changed recently with the introduction of some Macintosh clones. You can also find more third-party vendors selling Macintosh hardware.

Apple includes a complete line of systems; the clone makers offer similar systems.

Don't Buy a Discontinued Model Apple introduces newer models of each line quite frequently. When a company introduces a new model, they may discontinue an older model. Some products have short lives—less than one year. A dealer, though, may still have older models in stock. When you purchase a Mac model, be sure to ask the dealer whether it is a discontinued model. You can also double-check by calling and asking Apple.

Apple used to offer a low-end model called the LC and a high-end model called the Quadra, but most Macs offered today are in the Performa line or the Power Macintosh line.

You can select from several different Performa models. Most offer 8 to 16MB of RAM, a 15-inch monitor, a 250MB to 1G hard drive, and a SuperDrive. Some models include a CD-ROM drive and a fax modem, in addition to different software bundles.

The Power Macintosh line was introduced in 1994 and includes a new type of microprocessor chip. The chip, developed jointly by Apple, IBM, and Motorola, uses a different technology (RISC or Reduced Instruction Set Computing) that is less expensive to manufacture and is more powerful than the current Motorola and Intel chips. The computer also has the added advantage of being able to run Macintosh, DOS, and Windows applications on the same computer.

The Power Macintosh models are comparable to the Pentium models offered for PCs. You can select speeds from 100 to 132 MHz. Most models come with 16MB or more of RAM and a 1G or 2G SCSI hard drive.

The critical factor for this type of computer is that currently the software that is available doesn't take advantage of the powerful features of the chip. For the chip to be a viable contender, it has to have market support.

If you want to be on the cutting edge of technology, you may want to consider this type of PC.

In addition to the desktop models, Apple also offers a line of portable computers called PowerBooks. These portables weigh around six to seven pounds and are 2.3 × 11.3 × 9.3 inches or less in size. All models include a built-in trackball.

You can also purchase a PowerBook Duo, a combination portable and desktop system. You can take the portable with you or slide the portable into the docking station (a regular-sized desktop computer with system unit, keyboard, and monitor) and use the desktop unit.

Macintosh Printers

In addition to computer systems, Apple also manufactures a line of printers: dot-matrix printers (ImageWriters), inkjet printers (StyleWriters) and laser printers (LaserWriters). All the information on printers in Lesson 11 applies to Apple printers.

Although this book covers mostly PCs, you can use the information to select the hardware and software you need. The criteria for deciding what you need is the same.

Lesson 16

Buying a Portable Computer

In this lesson, you will learn about the different types of portable computers. If you want to purchase a portable, you can use this chapter to help you select a good system.

What Is a Portable Computer?

A *portable computer* is a computer that you can carry around. You could, if you want, lug your desktop computer around, but that's not going to be very easy. To make it easy to take a computer with you, computer designers keep creating smaller and smaller computers. Each time a company designs a new or smaller computer, the computer receives a new category name. The next section helps you understand names like *portable*, *notebook*, and *subnotebook*.

Types of Portables

As technology becomes more and more advanced, the size of a computer becomes smaller and smaller. Here's a rough timeline of the development of the portable computer:

- The original "portable" computer was similar to a desktop model but the monitor and system unit were combined. The computer, sometimes called a luggable, included a carrying case and was heavy— it weighed over 15 pounds.

- *Laptops* were the next generation of portable computers. These computers weighed nine to 12 pounds.

- The *notebook* computer was smaller than the laptop. These popular computers are around 8 1/2 × 11-inches in dimension and weigh as little as four to six pounds. You can fit a notebook computer inside your briefcase.

- If you want a computer smaller than a notebook, you can purchase a *subnotebook* or *handbook*. These computers weigh around two to three pounds.

- Another type of computer, about the size of a checkbook, is the *palmtop* or *organizer*. These computers usually include a day planner, calculator, and other features. You can also buy software to run on the palmtop. The keyboard is very cramped, and there is a limit of the processing power.

- A *pen computer* is a portable computer that uses a different technology for inputting information. Rather than type information, you use a pen to write on the screen. These computers most often have a specific purpose. For instance, the UPS person may use a pen computer to record your receipt signature for a package.

Do You Need a Portable?

You may want to consider purchasing a portable computer rather than a desktop model if you travel often. You can take a portable with you and use it in your office or home, on an airplane, or in a hotel. With communication features, you can use your portable computer to connect with other computers, for example, your home office.

If you have a desktop computer, but want to purchase another computer to use while you are away, you may want

Lesson 16

to purchase a portable computer. Using cables, you can transfer information from the desktop computer to your portable one.

Keep in mind that portable computers are usually more expensive than their desktop counterparts. You can get a better system for the money if you are purchasing a desktop computer.

Buying a Portable Computer

The size of a portable computer is different than a desktop model, but both types of computers work essentially the same way and have the same parts.

A portable computer, like a desktop computer, includes the following hardware:

- **A microprocessor.** Like desktop models, a portable also includes a microprocessor chip (refer to Lesson 6). You should get at least a Pentium chip in your portable. As for speed, 75MHz is probably acceptable. Keep in mind that you pay a premium for the design of the small system, so you aren't getting as much power for your money.

    > **SL Chips** Often used in portable computers because they offer power-saving features. These chips can turn off power to components that aren't being used.

- **RAM.** A portable computer also uses random-access memory, measured in megabytes. The more memory the better. You probably want at least 4MB if not 8MB for your portable.

- **Hard drive.** It's hard to believe a hard disk fits inside that tiny case, but it does. Like memory, you want the largest hard drive you can afford. 100MB is a good minimum size.

- **Floppy drive.** If you want to transfer information from one computer to another using disks, you need a floppy drive. You can also connect the two computers via a cable to transmit information. In this case, you don't need a floppy drive, but you need a special software program.

You can check these specs just as you would for a desktop model. Most portables will offer several systems that match the preceding list. The other components (size, monitor, keyboard, and battery life) make the difference in comparing laptops. The next sections discuss these topics.

Size

As mentioned earlier, portables differ in size. If you are deciding what type to purchase, you may want to let the size of the computer help you pick.

For example, if you have to carry the computer with you everywhere, you may want to select the lightest computer available. You can compare the weight of different types and models to select the one for you.

> **What's the Total Weight** Keep in mind that four pounds doesn't sound like much, but that's not the total weight. In addition to the computer itself, you are going to have to carry the case, extra batteries, and other equipment (battery charger, disks, and so on). Be sure to find out how heavy the entire package is—not just the computer itself.

In addition to the weight, you should check the dimensions of the computer—how big it is. If you are checking an ad, you may see the dimensions 9.75" × 5.9" × 1.6" (length, width, depth). If you visit a computer store, you can visually compare the sizes.

Screen Displays

Because the computer is smaller, the screen display is also smaller. Plus, the screen uses a different method for displaying an image on-screen: a liquid-crystal display. This type of display consists of a light panel and a layer of electrically charged liquid-crystal cells. These charged cells filter through one of three color filters so the color can appear on-screen.

The screen lights from the back (backlit) or side (side-lit). Backlit displays are brighter and better quality than side-lit ones. Also, the display may be black and white or color. Color is more expensive, as you may have expected. Color displays also require more processing power (see the section on batteries). Another factor is whether the matrix (the screen) is active or passive. Active is preferable.

When comparing screens, you will want to compare the size and the type of display (VGA, for example). You will also want to be sure that the screen tilts easily so that you can view it from different angles.

Keyboard and Pointer

The keyboard on a portable is also smaller than a regular desktop computer. Select one that is easy to type on; make sure the keys aren't too cramped and the keys have a good "feel" (not squishy or clicky).

In addition to a keyboard, the computer may include a pointing device, such as a trackball. This trackball may be integrated into the keyboard, or it may be a separate component that you attach with a clip. Integrated is better.

Battery

There are two types of rechargeable batteries that power portable computers: nickel-cadmium (NiCad) and nickel-metal-hydride (NiMH). NiCad batteries are cheaper; NiMH last longer.

Buying a Portable Computer

Bargain Shopper When you are purchasing a portable computer, ask the salesperson to throw in some extra equipment as part of the sale. For example, you can ask for a carrying case or an extra battery.

Because the battery powers every component of the computer, the battery may not last long (three hours is a good "working" time). When you purchase a portable, ask about the battery life. Also, ask how long it takes to recharge the batteries.

Expansion Capabilities

You can usually add functions, such as a modem or memory, through the use of a PCMCIA (Personal Computer Memory Card International Association) slot and card. There are three types of these slots/cards: memory cards usually use Type I, modem cards usually use Type II, and hard drives use Type III.

Check the Recommended Cards Before you purchase a card, check with the manufacturer of your portable. Not all cards work with all portables. Most manufacturers provide a list of acceptable cards.

Summary Checklist

Use this summary checklist to record the specs for the portable that matches your needs.

1. Type of processor: _____

2. Speed: _____

3. Memory: _____

Lesson 16

4. Hard disk size: _____

5. Dimensions: _____

6. Weight: _____

7. Monitor

　　Size: _____

　　❑ Monochrome　　❑ Color

　　❑ Backlit　　❑ Sidelit

　　❑ Active matrix　　❑ Passive matrix

8. Batteries

　　❑ NiCad　　❑ NiMH

　　Battery Life: _____

　　Recharge time: _____

9. PCMCIA Slots

　　❑ Type I

　　❑ Type II

　　❑ Type III

Lesson 17

Completing Your Computer Shopping List

In this lesson, you will learn how to create a comprehensive shopping list.

Selecting Software

When you purchase a new system, you may not think to include the price of software in your budget. However, without software, you won't be able to use your computer to do much. Therefore, you need to plan for the software you need.

First, make a list of what you need to get started. You need Windows 95, which should be included with the PC.

Second, make a list of software you will need later. It's probably a good idea to start with one application and then add others as you become familiar with the computer. If you start with five programs, you are likely to feel overwhelmed and end up not using the computer at all. Start with one or two programs and then add the others gradually. However, you should at least have an idea of other software applications you will want to add.

Lesson 17

Third, once you have a list of the software you know you need, jot down the system requirements for those programs. You will want to buy a computer system that can run the software you want.

Use the summary checklist at the end of this lesson to record your software list.

Selecting Hardware

It will help you when you go shopping for a computer to have a particular system in mind, that is, the type of microprocessor, range of speed, amount of memory, and so on. If you've been making notes up to now, you should have a good idea of what you want. The summary checklist at the end of this lesson pulls together all the system information.

If you still don't have any idea, you can use the following list of minimum recommendations to help you select a system.

Minimum System Recommendation

Pentium, 75MHz+

800MB hard drive

8-16MB RAM

At least one 3.5-inch drive

SuperVGA or VGA monitor: noninterlaced, .28mm dot pitch, 14-inch, 1MB memory

At least one parallel port and two serial ports

At least four expansion slots

This general purpose computer will run most major application programs.

Setting a Budget

One thing that we need to discuss is money. It usually isn't a good idea to let your budget dictate the type of computer you purchase. Suppose that you have only $1,200 to spend on a computer that you want to use to automate all of your sales and office information. You purchase a complete system (computer, monitor, printer, modem, software) for $1,200, and think you got a good deal.

However, when you try to use your computer to do what you want, you find out that you can't automate sales because the program you need won't run on your system. You can't print out the sales presentations because the printer is a cheap dot-matrix printer, and the printouts look unprofessional. You bought a modem, but you don't really need it. And the software that came with your package isn't what you need either. You then have to consider whether you did indeed get a good deal.

It's better to go with what you need and see how much that setup is going to cost. If the price is too high, you can then decide whether to spend the extra money or decide where you need to cut back. For instance, you may find the complete system you *want* costs $2,500. You may decide to pay the additional amount to get this system. Or you may decide not to purchase all the items at once. For example, you may decide that you don't need the modem just yet; you can buy it later.

The following summary checklist includes a column for pricing. You can use this to help you figure out a budget for your "ideal" system. Then you can make the "ideal" system match your budget.

Summary Checklist

You can use this checklist in one of two ways. First, you can use it to record the equipment you need. When you go shopping, compare systems on the market to your list and then find the one that matches most closely. Second, you can make copies of this list and then complete the information for each system that you look at. After you've collected all this information, you can go back and select the "best" system by comparing the information.

Software

1. Check the software you need. If the software comes with the system package, check the Included box. If it isn't, write in the price. If you know the specific software product you want, write it in the space below the software type.

Need	Program	Included/Price
❑	Word Processing Program _____	❑/_____
❑	Spreadsheet Program _____	❑/_____
❑	Database Program _____	❑/_____
❑	Financial Program _____	❑/_____
❑	Integrated Program _____	❑/_____
❑	Graphics Program _____	❑/_____
❑	Desktop Publishing Program _____	❑/_____

Completing Your Computer Shopping List   **123**

Need	Program	Included/Price
❑	**Utility Program** _____	❑/_____
❑	**Other** _____ _____ _____ _____	❑/_____

2. Record any software requirements that you need to be sure to match:

Software program	_____
Operating system required	_____
Processor required	_____
Amount of memory (RAM)	_____
Amount of hard disk space	_____
Type of monitor	_____
Other requirements	_____
Type of disk	_____
SOFTWARE TOTAL	$_____

Hardware

1. Check the type of microprocessor:

❑ 80486DX

❑ 80486DX2

❑ Pentium

Lesson 17

2. Check the speed of the microprocessor:

❑ 75 MHz

❑ 100 MHz

❑ 120 MHz

❑ 133 MHz

3. Check the amount of memory or RAM:

❑ 4MB

❑ 8MB

❑ 16MB

❑ 32MB

Can you add memory?   ❑ Yes   ❑ No

4. Check the size of the hard disk:

❑ 400 to 800MB

❑ 800MB to 1G

❑ 1G+

Access time: _____

Controller type: _____

5. Check the floppy disk drives:

❑ 3 1/2-inch

❑ 5 1/4-inch

6. Check the type of monitor:

  ❑ VGA

  ❑ SuperVGA

  Size: _____

  Resolution: _____

  Amount of RAM: _____

  Type of bus _____

7. Type of keyboard? _____

8. Check the type of mouse:

  ❑ Serial

  ❑ Bus

  Manufacturer: _____

9. Number of ports:

  _____ Parallel

  _____ Serial

10. Expansion slots

Number of slots	Type
_____	_____
_____	_____
_____	_____
_____	_____

  SYSTEM TOTAL $_____

11. Check the type of printer:

❑ Dot-matrix

❑ 9-pin

❑ 24-pin

   Resolution: _____

❑ Inkjet

   Resolution: _____

   Speed (pages per minute) _____

❑ Laser

   Resolution: _____

   Speed (pages per minute) _____

12. Check any other hardware that you need or that is included in the system:

Need	Hardware	Included/Price
❑	Modem	❑/_____
❑	Fax modem	❑/_____
❑	Tape backup	❑/_____
❑	CD-ROM drive	❑/_____
❑	Sound card	❑/_____
❑	Joystick	❑/_____

OTHER HARDWARE TOTAL $_____

Lesson

Doing Some Research

In this lesson, you will learn about some resources you may want to investigate to help you make a purchase decision.

Reading Magazines

If you open a computer magazine and try to read it, you might think that you have stumbled onto a secret world. You may see headlines such as "Pentiums Speed Up to 100MHz" or "Triple Speed: Faster than a DX2-66, Cheaper than Pentiums." You can't use the magazines *alone* to figure out what type of PC to buy. You first need to understand the lingo.

This book should help you do that. Using this book, you should know or be able to look up terms such as MHz, Pentium, or 486. Then you can use the magazines as a research tool.

Selecting a Magazine

There are many computer magazines on the market. If you go to a bookstore or a local newsstand, you will probably see some of the more popular ones stocked—for example, *PC World*, *PC Computing*, *PC Magazine*, and so on. There's no real test to decide which magazine is best. Most magazines include similar features (reviews, feature stories, news stories, and so on) and cover similar topics.

The best way for you to decide which magazine you like is to flip through it. Which magazine looks easier to use? Which articles sound interesting? Is the writing style easy to understand or is it "techie?" Pick the one you like the best.

Getting the Most from the Magazine

Once you select a magazine, you probably won't want to read it cover to cover. You'll probably find that the reviews are long and include all sorts of technical specs, such as charts showing the time it takes each reviewed computer to open a 1-2-3 file. If you are doing a fine-tooth-comb comparison, you may find these details to be interesting. Otherwise, it's a good idea to look for generalities.

Here are some strategies for getting the most from the magazine:

- **Review the computer system advertisements.** Doing so will give you an idea of the type of systems available as well as the price. See the following "Decoding an Advertisement" section for information about making sense of the ads.

- **Review the software advertisements.** If you aren't sure what you want the computer to do, review the software ads. These will give you some idea of what you can do with your computer.

- **Read the review summaries.** Most magazines summarize the strengths and weaknesses of a system in the review. These summaries will give you a good idea of why you would or wouldn't want to buy a particular system.

- **Look for "editor's choice" or "best buy" seals.** Many magazines rate several systems and then select a few of the best, noting these with some type of "seal." If you aren't sure what type of computer to purchase, you might want to check magazines and see which brands they rate as a "best buy" or good choice.

- **Look for information on service or on a company's reputation.** Suppose that you have decided to purchase a computer by a particular manufacturer, but you want to make sure the system is reliable. You can look for reviews of products by that company and check the information on service and system problems.

Decoding a Computer Advertisement

When you are reviewing the magazine, you will probably notice ads for different systems. The following table shows sample lines from advertisements in the left column and shows what they actually mean in the right column.

Line in Ad	What It Means
P5-75	The product name for this particular computer.
Intel P5 75MHz	The microprocessor chip (Pentium) and the chip speed (75MHz). For more information on chips, see Lesson 6.
8MB RAM 256KB cache	The amount of memory (8MB) as well as the cache size. Lesson 6 covers memory and disk caches.
850MB 10ms EIDE	The size of the hard drive (850MB), access speed (10ms), and controller type (EIDE). Lesson 7 covers hard disks.
PCI Local Bus with 1MB	The type of video adapter and the amount of memory. Lesson 9 covers monitors.
4x EIDE CD-ROM	The speed (4x or quad speed) and controller type (EIDE) of the CD-ROM drive. Chapter 13 covers CD-ROM drives.

continues

Continued

Line in Ad	What It Means
3.5" Diskette Drive	The size of the floppy drive. Lesson 7 covers floppy drives.
15: .28 dp SVGA Monitor	Describes the size (15-inch), dot pitch, and type of monitor (SVGA). Lesson 9 covers monitors.
Desktop case	Describes the style of the system unit. Lesson 8 covers case styles.
4 ISA, 2 PCI slots	The number and type of expansion slots in the system unit case. Lesson 8 covers expansion slots.
AnyKey Keyboard MS Mouse	The type of keyboard and mouse. Lesson 10 covers keyboard and mice.
Microsoft Windows 95	Includes Windows 95.
$1899	The price of the system.

Once you understand the ads, you can compare different features and models.

Visiting Computer Stores

Another strategy for collecting information is to visit computer stores and take a look at the different types of computers offered. This section discusses some things you may want to consider doing on your visit.

Quizzing the Salesperson

If you have a knowledgeable salesperson, ask questions. In some stores, the salesperson may know less than you do about computers, so ask a few questions first to see what he knows. If you think the person understands computers pretty well, ask other questions. You may want to prepare a list of questions beforehand. For instance, if you don't understand the difference between a VESA bus and a local bus, ask the salesperson to explain. Ask what the benefits are of a particular component. Ask the salesperson which computer system he would recommend and why. Does the salesperson have a computer at home? If so, what type? Ask him which model is the most reliable.

Keep in mind that the person is probably going to pressure you into making a purchase. You should avoid making a purchase on your first visit to the store. Tell the salesperson you are "just looking."

Also, don't tell the salesperson how much money you want to spend. That's likely one of the first questions the salesperson will ask. Price is certainly a consideration, but you don't want to make a purchase based solely on price. You want a computer that will match your needs.

Picking Up Sales Literature

Many stores have a flyer printed for each system they offer. The flyer will probably list the "specs" and possibly the price. If they don't have flyers, they may have a catalog of products. Get a copy of any flyers and catalogs. You can then use the catalog to compare systems. First, be sure you understand all the "specs." If you don't understand something listed, ask. Second, compare prices.

Trying Out Systems and Software

When you are in the store, you should also try out different systems. Which monitor do you like? Which keyboard feels OK? Which computer looks and feels like a good product?

This step is especially important if you decide to purchase a computer through the mail. Stores may sell some mail-order brands. You can try them out at the store and then order through the mail if the mail-order price is better. (Lesson 19 gives more information about where to shop.)

You should also demo the software. If you are trying to decide which software package to purchase, ask for a demonstration of the various software packages. For example, suppose that you are trying to select a word processing package. You can ask to see the two most popular programs, then play around with the first program and see what you like and don't like. Is it intuitive? Do you like the interface?

> **What's an Interface?** An interface is what you see on-screen when you use a program. Some versions of WordPerfect display a blank screen when you start the program. Some people love this; some hate it. You should feel comfortable with the interface of the software you want to buy.
>
> *Plain English*

Next, try out the other program and compare it to the first one. Which do you prefer? One of the most important things in selecting hardware and software is to get something you are comfortable with. Sometimes, you will make a decision based on something intangible. One system will just *seem* better to you.

Soliciting Advice from Others

Another good way to get information is to ask other people that use computers what they prefer. Everyone will have an opinion, and those opinions may vary wildly. However, you can still get some good information. Here are some ideas for gathering information:

- **Ask your coworkers.** If you work in an office, ask your coworkers what they use and like. Ask them about any problems they've had. Ask them what type of system they would recommend and why.

- **Ask other people that work in your field.** If you don't have any coworkers or they don't use computers, ask other people that work in your field. For instance, if you are in the legal field, you may want to ask people in other law offices what type of system they have and what type of software they use. Again, ask them what they like and don't like about their setup.

- **Ask relatives.** There's probably someone in your family that has or knows something about computers. If so, ask for his experiences. What has worked for that person? What hasn't?

- **Visit computer meetings.** Many cities have computer societies: a group of members that may meet on a regular basis to discuss issues dealing with computing. The members of this organization may be able to provide you with some recommendations. Within the group, there may be individual user groups. For example, the computer group may have a user group for Word for Windows.

> **Help!** Check with your local library for computer groups and meetings.

In the end, you will have to weigh all the information you collect and then take the plunge. In the next lesson, you'll learn about different places you can shop for your computer.

Lesson 19

Deciding Where to Buy

In this lesson, you learn about the different places you can purchase a computer.

Where Computers Are Sold

As computers become more and more popular, the places that stock and sell them become more and more widespread. Just recently Wal-Mart started selling computers. You can purchase a computer at any of the following store types:

- Computer dealers
- Computer superstores
- Mail order
- Electronics stores
- Department and discount stores
- Local box maker

Like any store, computer stores vary in price, selection, and stock. The rest of this chapter discusses each of these places and gives you an idea of the advantages and disadvantages of shopping at each.

Computer Dealers

Before computers became widespread, they were initially for sale mostly through computer dealers. These small to medium-sized stores usually stocked a few brands of computers and other equipment. Although this type of store is still around, competition drove some computer dealers out of business.

The advantage of this type of store is usually the salespeople. Because the salespeople sell only computers, they are usually fairly knowledgeable. You can have the salesperson demonstrate different systems and software. This type of store also provides a range of services like training and support. A computer dealer may configure or set up your system (for example, install the software).

On the down side, you will probably pay a premium for the service you get at a computer store. Also, the store may carry only a limited selection of computers.

Visit a Computer Store Although you may not want to purchase your computer at a dedicated computer store, you may want to visit this type of store to collect information and gather advice.

Computer Superstores

In the early 1990s a new type of computer store opened: a computer superstore or warehouse. This type of store started in big cities, and then as they became successful, branched out to other cities. Some common stores are Elek-Tek, Computer City, and CompUSA.

This type of store is big and offers many computer systems and computer add-on products. Because they stock in quantity, you can usually get a good price. You can also purchase all your computer products (hardware, software, supplies, and so on) from one store. Another benefit is that you can demo the different systems to see which you like. Some superstores offer service, support, and training.

If you shop at this type of store, you should watch out for two things. First, be sure that you get a decent system.

Because they stock a variety, you can't be sure every computer system offered is top quality. Second, if you talk to a salesperson, be sure he is knowledgeable. These sales people may be not well-trained or well-versed in computer technology.

Mail-Order Vendors

If you flip through a computer magazine, you will notice there are many advertisements for mail-order computers. Many top-rated companies, such as Dell and Compaq, started out as mail-order companies. Now you can purchase Dell and Compaq computers through the mail or at a retail store. Other good companies, such as Gateway, remain strictly mail-order.

> **Use a Credit Card** If you purchase a computer through the mail, use a credit card to pay for the system. If you have problems receiving the computer, the credit card company can help mediate the dispute.

Mail-order companies can offer good prices because they don't have the overhead of storefronts and warehouses. If you know the type of computer you want, you can buy a mail-order system designed exactly to your specification. Most mail-order vendors also preconfigure your system (install the operating system, drivers, and software). Because you are buying the computer sight-unseen, most mail-order vendors have a liberal return policy. These are all pluses.

On the down side, keep in mind that you won't be able to try out the computer before you buy it, and the mail-order company only carries one line of systems. If you don't know what you want or think you need the added support or service of a local vendor, you may not want to purchase from a mail-order company.

Do Some Checking Be sure to check out the mail-order company: make sure that it has been in business for a while. Check computer magazines and the Better Business Bureau.

Electronics Stores

An electronics store stocks all kinds of products: washers, dryers, stereos, TVs, and computers. These types of stores range in size from a small-to-medium store to giant electronics warehouse stores.

You may be more comfortable shopping at this type of store because you can browse around through other more familiar equipment. Many of these stores advertise in the Sunday paper—usually complete computer systems. If you want a low-end complete system, you can purchase a bundle from this type of store.

If you decide to shop at an electronics store, keep in mind that it's unlikely you'll find a knowledgeable salesperson. Also, these stores may offer limited training, support, product selection, and service features. For example, the repair workers for that store may not know how to fix computers. If the computer needs work, the store may send it out for repairs. Be sure to find out who fixes your computer if you bring it in for repairs. If you need to ship the computer somewhere, ask who pays for shipping.

Beware Impulse Shoppers! You shouldn't purchase a computer system on a whim, which can be tempting as you browse through an electronics superstore. Before you purchase, you should do some research and compare systems and prices.

Department, Discount, and Office Supply Stores

In addition to computer and electronics stores, you may be able to purchase a computer at your local department store, a discount warehouse store (such as SAMS), a discount retail store (such as Wal-Mart), or an office supply store. Most of these stores will have a limited selection of computer systems. Usually, these stores sell the system as a bundle: system unit, monitor, printer, software, and add-ons.

If you shop at this type of store, you may be able to get a reasonably priced system, but be sure you are getting a quality system. Just because a wholesale club stocks a computer doesn't mean it is the best system for the money. The wholesale club may have purchased this model because it was inexpensive. Also, it's not likely that you will find expert salespeople or after-sale support (training, service, and so on) if you purchase your system from this type of store.

Local Box Makers

The pieces that make up a computer aren't just available to big computer makers. Any individual can purchase and put together a computer—if he or she knows how. There are many small companies that build custom-made PCs. You can order just the PC you want, and they will build it to your specifications. Usually the prices are low because the company has few advertising and overhead costs.

To find this type of vendor, check your Yellow Pages or ask a local computer users' group. This group might know of such a company. Be sure to check out the company's reputation.

Similar to buying from a mail-order vendor, you shouldn't buy from a local box maker if you don't know what you want or think you will need training or after-sale support.

In this lesson, you learned about different places to buy your computer. In the next lesson, you'll learn how to actually make the big purchase.

Lesson

Making the Purchase

In this lesson, you will learn how to make the final decision: select a particular brand of computer and check other information.

To Buy a Bundle or Not?

Many electronics stores or retail stores sell a computer system as a bundle. For one price, you get the system, monitor, keyboard, printer, and software. Sometimes, these stores will include additional hardware in the bundle, such as a modem or a CD-ROM drive. Usually the system has a reasonable price for a low-end system. This type of advertised system may tempt you to purchase it. After all, why fuss over several decisions when you can just make one decision—buy the whole kit and caboodle at once.

Buying a bundle, in some cases, can be a good idea. For example, if you are purchasing a home computer for your children, a bundle may be a good idea.

In most cases, you should carefully compare the bundle to your needs. Ask yourself these questions:

- **Is the system powerful enough?** Most systems included in a bundle are low-end machines. They may have a medium-size hard disk, less memory, and slower processor. Be sure you get a computer powerful enough for your needs.

Lesson 20

- **Is the printer acceptable?** Some bundles include a dot-matrix printer, others an inkjet. If you are getting a printer as part of the package, be sure it is the kind of printer you need. If you really need a laser printer, the dot-matrix printer included with the system isn't going to be of much use.

- **Do you need the other hardware included?** As mentioned, some bundles come with other hardware, such as a sound card, a CD-ROM drive, or a fax modem. If you *need* this equipment, then the bundle might be a good choice. If you don't need the equipment, you should consider whether you can spend the same amount and get a high-powered system.

- **Do you need the included software?** The sellers are going to make it appear as if you are getting the software for free. However, keep in mind that you are really paying for all the items included in the bundle—in some way or another. Be sure to weigh the value of the software as compared to your needs. If you won't use the software, it's not valuable.

- **Is the computer brand reliable?** Most bundles include a reliable computer brand, such as Acer or Packard Bell. To be on the safe side, you should check to be sure.

- **Are the warranty and service agreements okay?** The next section discusses how to check out a warranty. If you purchase a bundle, be sure to read that section and ask the appropriate questions.

Checking the Warranty, Service, and Support

When you are shopping for computer systems, you should check out the warranty, service, and support to be sure they are acceptable. Find out the following information:

Minimum Warranty The minimum warranty you should accept is one year, but two is better. Look for one that provides a year of on-site service and telephone technical support.

- **How long has the company been in business?** If the company goes out of business and your computer breaks down, the warranty isn't going to be helpful.

- **What's the money-back guarantee?** If you don't like the system, can you return it? Can you get a full credit? Some companies charge a restocking fee for the return. You should have a 30-day money-back guarantee and no restocking fee.

- **Who backs the warranty?** The vendor or the manufacturer? Both should back it.

- **How long is the warranty?** One year is okay; two is better.

- **If you have a problem, where do you take the computer?** Will the repair person come to your site and fix the problem? (This type of service is called on-site.) Or do you have to bring the computer to the vendor? Or ship it back to the manufacturer? If shipping is involved, who pays? On-site service is best. If you have to ship the computer, the vendor or manufacturer should pay.

- **If a part breaks, will the company repair or replace it?** It's better to have the part replaced. First, the original part has already broken once. Second, you can get a replacement much faster than you can have the part repaired.

- **Will the vendor set up the system?** Setting up the system involves formatting the hard drive, installing the operating system, installing any other programs, and installing drivers (programs that enable the mouse, printer, and other equipment to work). If the vendor sets up your system, you will save yourself the time and trouble. Plus, you will be sure the system and all its components are working together.

- **Who do you call if you have a problem?** Will the company handle your calls promptly? Will the company charge you for calls? Ideally, you want a free 24-hour telephone line for support.

Comparing Systems

After reading this book, you may feel confident that you know the system you want. For example, you may decide you want a Pentium with 16MB RAM and an 800MB hard drive. Unfortunately, that's only half of the decision. Now you have to select *which* system to purchase. Many manufacturers offer similar or comparable models, with all the features you need and want. How can you decide?

This section discusses some strategies for making the final decision—which exact brand to purchase.

Buy Based on Price

If you are considering two equal computer systems and one is cheaper than another, you may want to purchase based on the price of the systems. Buying on price is an acceptable strategy as long as you are sure the two systems are comparable. Do they both offer similar components and power?

Are both manufacturers reputable? Are the warranties and service agreements similar?

Buy Based on Reputation

If you watch TV or read mainstream magazines, you may see advertisements for some of the major computer manufacturers, such as Compaq, IBM, or Apple. These companies have been in business since the advent of personal computers and have a good reputation. If reputation is important to you, then you may consider this strategy. However, you need to consider a few other things:

- **Are you paying extra for the brand name?** And if so, is it worth the value? Because they advertise heavily, major companies usually have more overhead than smaller companies, and they may charge a premium for their system. You need to decide if that premium is worth it.

- **What is the company's reputation?** A company may build a reputation on strong products, good service, market presence, and so on. If you are buying on reputation, be sure you are not buying on marketing hype. Ask yourself whether the company makes *better* PCs and if the company provides *better* service.

Buy Based on Recommendations

Another way to select a particular brand of computer is to ask coworkers, friends, family, and other people that work in your field. If a person has used a computer, they can and will usually relate their experiences. For example, a person may tell you that she loves her Gateway and hasn't had any trouble with it. Another person may tell you that the system he bought has been trouble since day one.

You can also ask salespeople for their recommendations, but consider their motives. Perhaps the salespeople have an incentive to sell that brand.

Call Computer Repair Centers As a spot check, you may want to call some local computer repair centers and ask what their experience has been with a particular brand. Do they see a lot of problems with that type of machine? Have they heard of any problems?

Buy What You Know

If you use a computer at your office and are happy with it, you may want to purchase the same type of system. You will most likely know what you like and dislike about the system. Having the same type of computer at your office and home will make it easy to get used to the home computer.

If you are purchasing a computer for your children and they use a particular computer at school, you may want to purchase the same kind.

Buy Based on Warranty, Service, or Support

Three areas where computer manufacturers will vary are with warranty, service, and support. If you are considering two similar systems, you should compare these areas. For example, does one brand offer a longer warranty? Does one warranty cover more components?

If the computer has problems, where do you send it? For some companies, you have to ship the computer somewhere. Or you take it to the shop, and they ship it somewhere. Other companies, on the other hand, provide on-site service. If something happens to your system, they will come to your location and fix it.

What support does the company offer? Do they have a number you can call if you have questions? Do they offer training? Will they set up your system for you?

Making the Purchase 145

Try the Support Number Try calling the support number to see first whether you can get through. Sometimes, the calls are so backlogged that the line is forever busy. If you do get through, is the person helpful and cheerful?

Buy Based on Look and Feel

Sometimes, the final decision will come down to the look and feel of the system. You may like the shape or design of one computer over another. The keyboard might feel better on one model. Or you may like the included software in the bundle better than another model. Generally, you'll do well to purchase a computer that you feel comfortable with.

Summary Checklist

Use this summary checklist to record the warranty and service you expect or to compare the warranties of systems you are considering.

1. Length of the warranty: _____

2. Check the company responsible for servicing the warranty:

    ❏ Vendor

    ❏ Manufacturer

    ❏ Third-party contractor

3. If the computer has problems, how is it handled?

    ❏ Sent back to manufacturer by you

    ❏ Sent back to manufacturer, but vendor or manufacturer pays

    ❏ Taken into store

    ❏ Service technician comes to you

Lesson 20

4. If a part is defective, how it is handled?

- ❏ Repaired
- ❏ Replaced

5. Does the vendor set up the computer?

- ❏ Yes
- ❏ No

Lesson 21

After the Sale

In this lesson, you will learn how to set up your computer system. This lesson also discusses some do's and don'ts to consider when using the computer.

Setting Up the Computer

When you purchase your new computer, you will need to unpack it and set it up in a good location. To do so, follow these steps:

1. **Unpack the computer system.** The computer system may come in two or three big boxes. Unpack the components carefully. After you unpack, check the invoice to be sure you received all the equipment you bought. If something is missing, contact the vendor immediately.

2. **Save the invoice, warranty information, and packing.** Save the invoice for your records. After you buy the computer, you may forget which type microprocessor you have or how much memory. The invoice should show a record of each component. You also need to record any serial numbers.

> **Keep a Computer Notebook** It's a good idea to keep a notebook or folder with all your invoice, warranty, and product information in one spot.

Complete and send in the warranty information. Save the packing so that if for some reason you have to return the computer, you have the original packing.

3. Pick a good location for your computer. Have plenty of desktop space for all the components (printer, monitor, keyboard, and mouse). Be sure that the cables can reach from the system unit to the monitor and from the system unit to the printer. You need a power source close by so that you can plug in the equipment.

Also, check the ventilation. A computer can generate a lot of heat. (That's why the system unit includes a cooling fan.) Place the computer so that air can circulate around all sides.

Finally, check the lighting. Make sure you can see the monitor without a glare.

4. Unpack and connect the system. You need to hook up the monitor, keyboard, mouse, and printer to the back of the system unit. Sometimes, the appropriate ports on the back of the system unit include the name; for example, the keyboard port may say "Keyboard." If they don't, you may be able to tell from the shape and size of the cables. Or you can check your computer system documentation to find out how to connect the equipment.

5. Plug in the components. The monitor, system unit, and printer all have separate power cords. You need to plug in these items. For your convenience, you may want to use a power strip so that you can plug in all three into one unit. Better yet, use a surge protector or surge suppressor.

6. Turn on the computer, monitor, and printer.
If you have a PC, you should see Microsoft Windows. If you have a Macintosh, you see the Macintosh desktop.

> **Nothing Happens?** If nothing happens when you turn on the computer, unplug all the components then connect them properly. (You shouldn't mess with the connections when the computer is on.) If you are using a power strip, be sure it is on. Check the monitor contrast or brightness. If still nothing happens, call your vendor for help.

Do's and Don'ts

Now that you have purchased and set up the computer, you are ready to start reaping the benefits of having a computer. Having a computer opens a wide world of existing possibilities. You can use your computer to do just about anything you want.

As you learn your way around the computer, keep in mind this list of do's and don'ts:

- **Do take your time.** Learning anything new doesn't happen overnight. If you are brand new to computers, give yourself some time to learn how to use it. At first, you may feel frustrated, but as you do more and more work on the computer, it will become easier and easier.

- **Don't be intimidated.** For the most part, there's nothing you can do to make the computer blow up. The equipment is pretty sturdy and can endure most user mistakes.

- **Don't jar or drop the computer.** Okay, it won't blow up, but the computer is still a fragile piece of equipment. (If you bump it, you probably aren't going to hurt it.)

- **Do keep magnets away.** Computers use a magnetized medium (your disks) to store information. Other magnets can wreak havoc if you put them on or near the disks. Be on the lookout for items you may not think of as magnetized, such as paper clips that are stored in a magnetized paper clip holder.

- **Don't attach equipment while the computer is on.** If you want to connect a piece of equipment to the computer, make sure you turn it off first. For example, if you are connecting a printer, turn off the computer and printer before you do any connecting.

- **Do use a surge protector.** Power surges can destroy data that you store on your computer, so it's a good idea to use some type of surge protection. You may want to purchase a power supply with surge protection, or you may want to purchase a surge protector.

- **Don't turn off the computer while you are running a program.** Before you turn off the computer, you should be sure to save anything that you are working on and then exit all programs. You should turn off the computer only after using the Shut down command.

- **Do keep a computer notebook or folder.** First, be sure to keep your computer purchase material organized. You should keep serial numbers, warranty information, invoice, and system information together in one spot. If you need technical support, you will most likely need access to this information. For instance, the service rep may ask you what type of monitor you have or what port you hooked up your mouse to.

After the Sale

- **Do keep your disks safe.** Keep your floppy disks in a safe, dry place. Keep them out of extreme heat or cold. Also, it's a good idea to label your disks so that you know what they contain.

- **Do organize your hard disk.** You can divide your hard disk into directories (similar to folders) and keep related information together. For example, you may want to keep all memos in one directory (folder). If you don't keep the files organized, you'll have a hard time finding anything. You can use Windows to create directories, as described in your Windows manual.

- **Do save your work.** When you are creating a document (for example, typing a memo), the computer temporarily stores the information in its memory. If the power goes out by accident or if you turn off the computer, you will lose any data stored in memory. For this reason, you need to save your work. When you save your work, the computer copies the work from memory to the hard disk. You should save every 5 or 10 minutes as you work. Also, before you exit a program, you should save your work.

- **Do back up your work.** A hard disk is a semi-permanent storage place. That means, for the most part, information you store on the hard disk is safe. However, hard disks can fail. Or more likely, users can make mistakes and delete files they need. To safeguard your data, you should make a backup copy and store the backup someplace safe. You should back up on a regular basis.

> **FYI** Windows 95 provides a backup program. You can also purchase a separate backup program.

- **Don't share software.** When you install a software program, you are basically copying the files from the floppy disks to the hard disk. The floppy disks still contain the files. You can use these disks again if something happens to the program. That doesn't mean that you can share the program files with someone else. Doing so is illegal. You can use software that you purchase only on your computer.

- **Do investigate classes or other books.** Most local colleges offer courses on using a computer or on using a particular program. You may want to take a course—especially if you are new to computers. Also, there are many books available to help you learn how to use the computer as well as any programs you might have purchased. Que, for example, publishes a complete line of computer books designed for different levels of users.

- **Do have fun.** You may have purchased the computer for a business reason, but don't forget that the computer can also be a vehicle for fun. You may want to take a break from the work and play a card game on the computer, or hook up and chat with other users on an on-line service. Keep in mind that you'll get the most from your computer if you enjoy using it.

Using a computer opens a wide world of exciting possibilities. With a computer, there is always something new to explore. Good luck, and enjoy!

Appendix A

Glossary

application A software program that enables you to do something or create something; for example, you can create documents with a word processing application, work with numbers with a spreadsheet application, and so on.

backup An extra copy of your data and/or program files. If something happens to the original, you can use the backup copy.

baud The rate which a signal between two modems changes in one second.

BIOS Stands for Basic Input/Output System. It is the software permanently recorded on the ROM chip. This software is what enables the computer to start itself.

bit Short for binary digit. The smallest bit of information a computer can process.

bits per second (bps) A measurement of the speed of a modem. Sometimes mistakenly called baud.

Bulletin Board System (BBS) A communication system set up usually by an individual and usually dedicated to a hobby or interest. You can connect to the BBS to chat with other BBS participants, download files, and more.

bus The electronic pathway that connects different components of the system together.

byte 8 bits or roughly one typed character.

cache A trick used for speeding up the computer. The computer makes assumptions about what data it thinks you will need and *stashes* the instructions in the cache.

Appendix A

CD-ROM Stands for Compact Disc-Read Only Memory. It's a storage device that stores a lot of information, such as an entire set of encyclopedias.

CGA An out-dated monitor standard. Stands for Color Graphics Adapter.

CISC Stands for complex instruction-set computing. The type of architecture used in Intel-based chips and most Motorola chips.

clip art Graphic pictures stored in electronic files that you can open and insert in a document.

compatible A type of computer that is the same as an IBM PC, but is manufactured by someone other than IBM.

CPU The main computer chip or set of chips. Stands for central processing unit. CPUs are named mostly with numbers (8088, 8086, 80286, 80386, 80486, Pentium). Also called the microprocessor.

database A type of application used for working with sets of information, such as an inventory, client list, and so on.

desktop publishing program A type of application used for page layout.

DOS Stands for Disk Operating System and pronounced "doss" (rhymes with boss). MS-DOS (Microsoft's product) is the most common operating system for IBM and compatibles. The most current version (at the time of this writing) is MS-DOS 6.22.

DOS prompt The on-screen prompt you see when you start the computer or have exited all programs. The DOS prompt usually looks like this: C:\>.

dot-matrix printer A type of printer that creates characters by striking a series of dots (which combine to create a character) against the ribbon.

dot pitch   A measurement of how close the holes are placed on a monitor. The laser beam that creates the image must pass through the holes. The closer the hole, the better the image. Dot pitch is measured in millimeters (mm).

dots per inch (dpi)   A measurement of the quality of a printer or monitor. The higher the number, the better quality the output.

download   The process of copying a file from a BBS or on-line service to your computer.

DX   A suffix added to a microprocessor number. DX chips are faster and more powerful than SX chips.

EGA   An out-dated monitor standard. Stands for Enhanced Graphics Adapter.

EISA   A 32-bit bus used in some computers. (See bus.) Stands for Extended Industry Standard Architecture.

ESDI   A fast, acceptable type of hard drive controller. Stands for Enhanced Small Device Interface.

expansion card   An electronic card that you insert in an expansion slot to add capabilities to your system.

expansion slot   A slot in the motherboard that enables you to add and connect expansion boards. These boards provide additional features, such as sound.

fax modem   A combination fax and modem. You can use this type of modem to send faxes from your computer to another computer or to a regular fax machine. You can also receive faxes.

floppy disk   A portable storage device. You insert a floppy disk into the floppy drive to gain access to the information on the disk. Disks come in two sizes (3 1/2-inch and 5 1/4-inch).

floppy drive   An opening on the front of the system unit that enables you to insert and access information on a floppy disk.

gigabyte   About 1 billion bytes.

graphics program   A type of application for creating graphic images. There are different types of graphics programs; for example, presentation programs for creating visual presentations, CAD programs for creating architectural and manufacturing drawings, paint and draw programs for creating pictures or logos, and so on.

hard disk   A storage device for files and programs. Hard disks come in different capacities, measured in megabytes.

hardware   The physical components, such as your monitor, keyboard, and system unit, that make up a computer.

IDE   An acceptable type of hard drive controller. Stands for Integrated Device Electronics.

inkjet printer   A type of printer that creates characters by spraying ink through tiny jets.

integrated program   A type of program that combines the most common applications (word processing, spreadsheet, charting, database, communication, and graphics) into one package.

Intel   The manufacturer of microprocessor chips used in IBM and IBM-compatibles.

ISA   A 16-bit bus used in many computers. Stands for Industry Standard Architecture.

joystick   An arcade-style input device often used to play games.

keyboard   A computer component with alphanumeric characters and other special keys that is used to communicate with the system unit.

kilobyte (K or KB)   1,024 bytes, usually rounded to 1,000 bytes. Abbreviated KB or K. Memory and file size are measured in kilobytes.

laptop   A type of portable computer that weighs around nine to 12 pounds.

laser printer A type of printer that creates an image similar to a photocopying machine. Laser printers provide the best quality for printouts.

math coprocessor A chip added to speed up arithmetic functions. A 486DX has a built-in math coprocessor.

MCA A 16- or 32-bit bus used in IBM computers. Stands for MicroChannel Architecture. See also *bus*.

Megabyte (M or MB) One million bytes. Bytes are a measure of computer information; memory and hard disk space is measured in bytes, usually megabytes. Abbreviated M or MB.

megahertz (MHz) The measurement of the speed of the microprocessor. Speeds range from 25MHz to 100MHz.

MFM An out-of-date type of hard drive controller. Stands for Modified Frequency Modulation.

microprocessor The main chip or "brain" of the computer. Sometimes called the CPU.

Microsoft Windows A graphical user interface that runs on top of DOS and provides a user-friendly way to communicate with your computer.

modem Stands for MOdulator-DEModulator. A peripheral device that enables you to communicate with other computers through the phone line.

monitor The essential output device. The monitor displays what you type.

motherboard The main circuit board inside the system unit. The motherboard contains the microprocessor chip.

Motorola The manufacturer of microprocessor chips used in Macintosh computers.

mouse An input device that you can use to select commands and items on-screen.

multimedia The combination of text, graphics, and audio to present a message.

Appendix A

Multimedia PC (MPC)   A multimedia PC includes a CD-ROM drive, a sound card, and speakers. Multimedia applications can play sounds and display animation and video stills.

multisync   A monitor that can operate using different video display standards.

notebook   A type of portable computer small enough to fit into a briefcase and weighing around four to six pounds.

on-line service   A professionally run BBS system that you can hook up to using your modem. You can review information (current events, sports scores, stock prices), send messages to other users, shop, make travel arrangements, download files, and more.

operating system   The software that directs your computer: tells it where to find a file, how to display a file, and so on. The most common operating system for IBM computers is MS-DOS.

palmtop   A portable computer about the size of a checkbook, usually with a limited function.

PCI   A 32-bit bus type introduced in 1993. This bus offers more features and more power than other bus types. Stands for Peripheral Component Interconnect.

PCMCIA (Personal Computer Memory Card International Association)   A slot and/or card you can use to add functions to a portable computer, such as more memory.

pen computer   A portable computer that uses a pen for an input device.

Performa   A mid-range line of Mactintosh computers.

pixel   The smallest unit that can be used to create an image. Short for picture element. Resolution for monitors is measured in pixels (for example, 640 × 480 is a standard resolution).

port   A plug on the back of the computer that enables you to hook up devices, such as a printer, to the computer.

Glossary

PowerBook A portable computer created by Apple.

PowerPC A type of microprocessor introduced in 1994 jointly by IBM, Apple, and Motorola. This chip uses a RISC technology for working with computer tasks. See RISC.

RAM Stands for random-access memory. It is a temporary storage space for information you are currently working on.

resolution A measurement of the crispness of a monitor image or a printed image.

RISC Stands for reduced instruction-set computing. It is the type of design used in the new PowerPC chip. This type of chip breaks down tasks into smaller tasks and is more powerful and cheaper than CISC chips. The CISC chip tries to handle the entire task at once.

ROM A type of memory that has instructions hard-coded on the chip. You cannot change the instructions in ROM (read-only memory).

scanner An input device that converts a printed image to an electronic image. Often used when working with graphics.

SCSI A type of controller. Stands for Small Computer Systems Interface and pronounced "SCUZ-zy." You can chain different SCSI devices together. Most Macintosh computers have at least one SCSI port.

SIMMs Stands for Single In-Line Memory Modules. TheY are chips that you can plug into your motherboard to add more memory.

software Instructions that tell your computer what to do; means the same as program or application. There are different types of software, including system software and application software.

sound card An electronic board added to your computer to provide sound capabilities.

spreadsheet A type of application used for working with numbers (calculating a budget, tracking sales, and so on).

subnotebook A smaller version (two to three pounds) of a notebook computer.

SuperDrive A 1.44MB floppy drive found standard in most Macintosh computers.

SuperVGA or SVGA The newest monitor standard. It can display 256 colors simultaneously.

SX A suffix added to a microprocessor number. SX chips are scaled-down versions of DX chips.

System The name of the operating system used on Macintosh computers. The current version is System 7.1.

system unit The case that houses the electronic parts (motherboard, memory, power supply, hard disk, floppy disk) of the computer.

trackball An input device (like an upside down mouse) used for issuing commands. Many notebook computers use a trackball.

utility A type of application program used for maintaining and tweaking your computer system.

VESA A 32-bit bus type introduced in 1993. This bus is an inexpensive bus type that provides more power than the ISA bus. It stands for Video Electronics Standards Association. It's also called the VL bus.

VGA An acceptable monitor standard. It can display 256 colors simultaneously.

word processing program A type of application used for working with words and for creating documents (memos, letters, reports, and so on.)

Index

Symbols

1-2-3 (Lotus Corporation), 24
3 1/2-inch disks, 55-56
5 1/2-inch disks, 55-56

A

accelerator cards (monitors), 69
Access (Microsoft Corporation), 25
accuracy (computers), 4-5
adapter cards (monitors), 66
add-ons, 37
adjusting monitors, 70
advertisements, 129-130
Altair 8800, 32
AMD (Advanced Micro Devices), 47
America Online, 88
Ami Pro (Lotus Corporation), 24
animation programs, 16
Apple I, 32
applications, 1-3, 10, 153
    backup programs, 151
    books, 104
    buying, 21-23
    communications, 17, 92-93
    databases, 14-15, 25
    desktop publishing, 17, 154
    disk compression, 53
    educational applications, 17-18
    fax applications, 92
    financial applications, 12-14, 24
    games, 18
    graphics, 15-16, 25, 156
    integrated applications, 17, 24, 156
    multimedia applications, 96
    spreadsheet applications, 12-14, 24, 160
    system requirements, 26
    utilities, 18, 160
    word processing, 10-12, 24, 160
architectural drawings, 16
audio capabilities, 99, 108-109

B

backups, 151-153
    disks, 57
    hard drives, 57
batteries (portable computers), 116-117
baud rate (modems), 89, 153
BBSs (bulletin board systems), 88, 153
benefits
    accuracy, 4-5
    businesses, 5-6
    organizational capabilities, 5
    time saving, 3-4
Bernoulli drives, 57
binary numbering system, 31
BIOS (Basic Input/Output System), 49, 153
bit widths (expansion slots), 59
bits, 153
boards, *see* cards
books, 104, 152
bps (bits per second) (modems), 153

brand names, 140, 143
brightness (monitors), tuning, 69-70
bubblejet printers, 82
budgets, 12-14
bundled computer systems, 139-140
bundled software packages, 21
bus mouse, 75
buses, 153
   EISA buses, 155
   expansion slots, 60
   ISA buses, 69, 156
   local video buses, 69
   MCA buses, 157
   microprocessors, 42, 46-47
   paths, 46
   PCI buses, 46, 61, 69, 158
   standards, 46
   VESA buses, 46, 61, 69, 160
business benefits, 5-6
buttons (mouse), 76
buying equipment
   budgeting purchases, 121
   bundled computer systems, 139-140
   CD-ROM drives, 100
   computer stores, 130-132
   hardware, 120
   Macintoshes, 106-111
   modems, 89
   multimedia PCs, 98-99
   printers, 78
   researching equipment
      advertisements, 129-130
      magazines, 127-130
      user groups, 133
      users, 132
   shopping lists, 121-126
   software, 21-23, 119-120
   sound cards, 99
   speakers, 99
bytes, 31, 48, 153

C

cables (printers), 78
caches (memory), 49, 153
CAD (computer-aided design) programs, 16
capacity (disks), 56
carbon forms, printing, 79
cards (expansion cards), 155
   inserting, 59
   memory cards, 117
   modem cards, 117
   ports, 62
   sound cards, 95, 159

   buying, 99
   compatibility with CD-ROM drives, 100
   cost considerations, 99
   video adapter cards, 66, 69
carpal tunnel syndrome, 74
cases (systems units), 62-63
CD-ROM drives, 57, 95, 100, 154
   CDs, 96
   Macintoshes, 107
CGA monitors, 68, 154
charts, 12-14
checkbook programs, 14
chips, see microprocessors
CISC (complex instruction-set computing) microprocessors, 154
ClarisWorks (Claris Corporation), 24
classes, 152
cleaning supplies, 104
clip art, 16, 154
closed architecture (Macintoshes), 109-110
color printers, 79
color monitors, 67
COM1 ports, 61
COM2 ports, 61
communications, 87
   BBSs (bulletin board systems), 88, 153
   faxes, 88
   modems, 89
      dialing computers, 87, 93
      external modems, 90-91
      fax modems, 91-92
      internal modems, 90-91
      speed, 89-90
   on-line services, 88, 158
   software, 17, 92-93
Compaq, 33, 136
compatibles, see PCs, IBM-compatibles
compressing
   disks, 53
   files, 90
CompUSA computer stores, 135
CompuServe, 88
Computer City stores, 135
computer furniture, 102-103
connecting
   equipment, 150
   modems to telephone lines, 93
contrast (monitors), tuning, 69-70
controllers, 53-54, 155-159
CorelDRAW! (Corel), 25
cost considerations, 6

Index

CD-ROM drives, 100
  Macintoshes, 36
  on-line services, 89
  PCs, 36
  portable computers, 114
  printers, 78, 80-83
  sound cards, 99
  speakers, 99
CPU (central processing unit), 154
  see also microprocessors
cursor movement keys, 73

D

databases, 14-15, 25, 154
dealers, 134
Dell mail-order company, 136
department stores, 138
desks, 102
desktop cases (system units), 62
desktop publishing programs, 17, 154
dialing computers, 87, 93
discount stores, 138
disk caches (memory), 49
disk compression programs, 53
disks, 55-56, 103, 155
  backups, 57
  CDs, 96
  compressing, 53
  disk holders, 104
  inserting in floppy drives, 54-55
  magnetic fields, 150
  software, 28
  temperatures for storing, 151
DOS (Disk Operating System), 9, 38-39, 154
dot pitch (monitors), 66, 155
dot-matrix printers, 79-80, 111, 154
downloading files, 155
  see also transferring files
dpi (dot per inch) (printers), 80-83
drawing programs, 16, 25
drive bays, 56
drivers (mouse), 76
drives
  Bernoulli drives, 57
  CD-ROM drives, 57, 95-96, 100, 107, 154
  drive bays, 56
  floppy drives, 54, 155
    Macintoshes, 107
    portable computers, 115
  hard drives, 52-53, 156
    backups, 57
    controllers, 53-54
    Macintoshes, 107
  organizing, 151
  portable computers, 114, 117
  optical drives, 57
  tape backup drives, 57
DX microprocessors, 45, 155

E

editing keys, 73
educational programs, 17-18
EGA monitors, 67, 155
EISA (Enhanced Industry Standard Architecture) buses, 46, 60, 155
electricity surge protectors, 103, 150
electronics stores, 137
Elek-Tek stores, 135
equipment, connecting, 150
ESDI (Enhanced Small Device Interface) controllers, 53, 155
Excel (Microsoft Corporation), 24
expansion cards, *see* cards
expansion slots, 59-60, 155
  Macintoshes, 108
  PCMCIA slots, 158
  portable computers, 117
external modems, 90-91

F

fax modems, 88, 91-92, 155
faxes, 88, 91-92
feeds (dot-matrix printers), 80
files
  backing up, 151
  compressing, 90
  saving, 151
  transferring, 87
financial programs, 12-14, 24
flat-bed scanners, 77
floppy disks, *see* disks
floppy drives, 54, 155
  inserting disks, 54-55
  Macintoshes, 107
  portable computers, 115
fonts (printer fonts), 81-83
Freelance Graphics (Lotus Corporation), 25
function keys, 72
furniture, 102-103

##

G (gigabytes), 48
games, 18
  joysticks, 77, 156
Gates, Bill, 32
Gateway mail-order company, 136

gigabytes, 48, 156
glare (monitors), 148
grammar checkers, 11
graphics (monitor display), 37
graphics programs, 15-16, 25, 156
graphs, 12-14
GUIs (graphical user interfaces), 38

H

hand-held scanners, 77
handbook computers, 113
hard drives, 52-53, 156
    backups, 57
    controllers, 53-54, 155-157
    Macintoshes, 107
    organizing, 151
    portable computers, 114, 117
    software system requirements, 27
hardware, 1-2, 30, 156
    buying, 120
    keyboards, 30, 72-74
    Macintoshes, 106-108
    modems, 30
    monitors, *see* monitors
    mouse, 30
    printers, *see* printers
    system unit, *see* system unit
Harvard Graphics (SPC), 25
help, 142-144
high-density disks, 56

I

IBMs, 32-34
    IBM PCs, 40
    IBM-compatibles, 33-34, 40-41, 154
    mainframes, 40
    software compatibility, 28
IDE (Integrated Device Electronics) controllers, 53, 156
inkjet printers, 81-82, 111, 156
input, 31
input devices
    joysticks, 77
    keyboards, 72-74
    mouse, 74-76
    scanners, 77
    track balls, 76
inserting
    cards into expansion slots, 59
    disks into floppy drives, 54-55
integrated programs, 17, 24, 156
Intel, 47, 156
internal modems, 90-91
inventories, 14
invoices, 147

ISA (Industry Standard Architecture) buses, 46, 60, 69, 156

J-L

Jobs, Steve, 32
joysticks, 77, 156

keyboards, 30, 72, 156
    keys
        cursor movement keys, 73
        editing keys, 73
        function keys, 72
        layout, 74
        program keys, 73
        tactility, 74
    Macintoshes, 107-108
    mapping, 73
    numeric keypads, 73
    portable computers, 116
    ports, 61
    wrist rests, 74
kilobytes, 47, 48, 156
knobs (monitors), 69-70

languages (laser printers), 84
laptops, 113, 156
laser printers, 83-84, 111, 157
layout of keyboard keys, 74
LCD (liquid-crystal display) monitors, 116
learning to use computer systems, 149-152
lighting considerations, 148
local box makers, 138
local video buses, 69
Lotus 1-2-3, 24
low-density disks, 56
LPT1 ports, 62

M

Macintosh LCs, 110
Macintoshes, 33-35, 106
    Apple I, 32
    buying, 106-111
    closed architecture, 109-110
    cost considerations, 36
    differences from PCs, 35
    discontinued models, 110
    drives, 107-108
    expansion slots, 108
    graphics capabilties, 37
    keyboards, 107-108
    learning to use, 36
    Macintosh LCs, 110

Index

memory, 106
microprocessors, 41
monitors, 107
mouse, 108
Performas, 110, 158
ports, 108
Power Macintoshes, 111
PowerBooks, 110-111, 159
Quadras, 110, 159
software, 28, 109
sound, 108-109
System operating system, 34, 39-40
upgrades, 37, 106
magazines, 127-130
magnetic fields, 150
mail-order vendors, 136-137
mailing lists, 14-15
mainframes, 40
manufacturing drawings, 16
mapping keyboards, 73
math coprocessors, 44, 157
MCA (Micro Channel Architecture) buses, 46, 61, 157
MDA monitors, 68
megabytes, 47-48, 157
megahertz, 157
memory
    caches, 49, 153
    laser printers, 83
    Macintoshes, 106
    portable computers, 114
    RAM, 47-48, 159
    ROM, 49, 159
    software requirements, 27
    video adapter cards, 69
memory cards (portable computers), 117
MFM (Modified Frequency Modulation) controllers, 53, 157
microphones, 95, 108
microprocessors, 31, 157
    68030 microprocessors, 106
    68040 microprocessors, 106
    80286 microprocessors, 33, 43-45
    80386 microprocessors, 33, 43-45
    80486 microprocessors, 33, 43-45
    8086 microprocessors, 43-45
    8088 microprocessors, 43-45
    Advanced Micro Devices, 47
    buses, 42, 46-47
    CISC, 154
    DX, 45, 155
    Intel, 47, 156
    math coprocessors, 44, 157
    megahertz, 157
    Moore's Law, 32, 43
    Motorola, 157
    Pentium microprocessors, 33, 44-45
    portable computers, 114
    PowerPCs, 33, 41, 44, 106-107, 159
    RISC, 111, 159
    software requirements, 27
    speed, 42, 45
    SX, 44-45, 160
    transistors, 31-32
Microsoft Access, 25
Microsoft Excel, 24
Microsoft Office, 21
Microsoft Windows, 9, 33, 157
Microsoft Word, 24
Microsoft Works, 24
modem cards (portable computers), 117
modems, 30, 87-91, 157
    baud rates, 153
    bps (bits per second), 153
    dialing computers, 87, 93
    fax modems, 88, 91-92, 155
    software requirements, 28
    telephone lines, connecting, 93
Money (Microsoft Corporation), 24
money-back guarantees, 141
monitors, 30, 65, 157
    adjusting, 70
    buses, 69
    CGA monitors, 68, 154
    EGA monitors, 67, 155
    glare, 148
    LCD (liquid-crystal display) monitors, 116
    Macintoshes, 107
    MDA monitors, 68
    multisync monitors, 158
    ports, 61
    resolution, 66, 159
        dot pitch, 66, 155
        pixels, 66, 158
        refresh rates, 66
    sizes, 68
    SVGA monitors, 67, 160
    tuning, 69-70
    VGA monitors, 67, 160
    video accelerator cards, 69
    video adapter cards, 66, 69
Moore's Law, 32, 43
motherboard, 49-50, 157
Motorola, 157
mouse, 30, 74-75, 157
    bus mouse, 75
    buttons, 76
    drivers, 76
    Macintoshes, 108

mouse pads, 103
ports, 61, 75
serial mouse, 75
software requirements, 28
tactility, 76
MS-DOS, 10, 32, 38-39
multimedia, 95-96, 157
multimedia PCs, 95-97, 158
 buying, 98-99
 standards, 97-98
multisync monitors, 158

N-O

NiCad (nickel-cadmium) batteries, 116
NiMH (nickel-metal-hydride) batteries, 116
NLQ (near letter quality) speed (dot-matrix printers), 80
notebook computers, 113, 158
numeric keypads, 73

OCR (optical character recognition) software (scanners), 77
office supply stores, 138
on-line services, 2, 88-89, 158
open architecture (PCs), 109
operating systems, 9-10, 158
 DOS, 9, 154
 MS-DOS, 10, 38
 PCs, 34
 software requirements, 27
 System, 9, 39-40, 109, 160
 Windows, 9, 38-39
optical drives, 57
organizational capabilities, 5
organizers, 113
organizing hard drives, 151
output, 31

P

packages (software), 21
pads (mouse pads), 103
Paintbrush (Microsoft), 25
painting programs, 15, 25
palmtop computers, 113, 158
paper (printers), 103
papers
 scanning, 77
 storing electronically, 5
Paradox (Borland), 25
parallel ports, 62
PC Computing magazine, 127
PC Magazine, 127
PC World magazine, 127

PCI (Peripheral Component Interconnect) buses, 46, 61, 69, 158
PCL printer language, 84
PCMCIA (Personal Computer Memory Card International Association) slots, 117, 158
PCs, 34-35
 Altair 8800, 32
 Apple I, 32
 cost considerations, 36
 differences from Macintoshes, 35
 graphics capabilities, 37
 IBM PCs, 32-34, 40
 IBM-compatibles, 33-34, 40-41, 154
 learning to use, 36
 multimedia PCs, 95-98, 158
 open architecture, 109
 operating systems, 34, 38-39
 popularity, 36
 portable computers, 112-114
 software compatibility, 28
 upgrades, 37
 see also IBMs; Macintoshes
Peformas (Macintoshes), 158
pen computers, 113, 158
Pentium microprocessors, 33, 44-45
Performas (Macintoshes), 110
phone lines, connecting modems, 93
photographs, scanning, 16, 77
pixels (monitors), 66, 158
plugging in computer systems, 148
pointing devices
 portable computers, 116
 see also mouse; track balls
portable computers, 112-117
 laptops, 112, 156
 notebook computers, 113, 158
 palmtop computers, 113, 158
 pen computers, 113, 158
 PowerBooks, 110-111, 159
 subnotebook computers, 113, 160
 weight, 115
ports, 61-62, 108, 158
PostScript printer language, 84
Power Macintoshes, 111
power strip, 103
power supply, 62
 batteries (portable computers), 116-117
 plugging in, 148
 power strip, 103
 surge protectors, 103, 150
PowerBooks (Macintoshes), 110-111, 159
PowerPC microprocessors, 33, 41, 44, 106-107, 159

PowerPoint (Microsoft Corporation), 25
presentations
    multimedia, 96
    programs, 15, 25
printer fonts, 81
printer stands, 102
printers, 30, 78
    bubblejet printers, 82
    cables, 78
    color printers, 79
    cost considerations, 78
    dot-matrix printers, 79-80, 154
    inkjet printers, 81-82, 156
    laser printers, 83-84, 157
    Macintosh printers, 111
    paper, 103
    ports, 61
    resolution, 83, 159
    stands, 102
printing carbon forms, 79
PrintShop (Broderbund), 25
processes, 31
ProComm Plus, 93
Prodigy, 88
program keys, 73
programs, *see* applications
prompts (DOS prompt), 154

Q

Q & A (Symantec), 25
Quadras (Macintoshes), 110, 159
queries (databases), 15
Quicken (Intuit), 24

R

RAM (Random Access Memory), 47-48, 159
    portable computers, 114
    upgrades, 48
    VRAM (video-RAM), 107
receiving faxes, 88, 91
recording sound (Macintoshes), 108
refresh rates (monitors), 66
remapping keyboards, 73
repairs, 141, 144
    product information, 147
    spare parts, 142
researching equipment
    advertisements, 129-130
    magazines, 127-130
    user groups, 133
    users, 132
resolution
    monitors, 66, 158-159
    printers, 80-83, 159
ribbons (dot-matrix printers), 80
RISC (Reduced Instruction Set Computing) microprocessors, 111, 159
ROM (Read-Only Memory), 49, 159
RSI (repetitive stress injury), 74

S

saving files, 151
scanners, 16, 77, 159
SCSI (Small Computer Systems Interface)
    controllers, 54, 159
    ports, 108
searching databases, 15
sending faxes, 88, 91
serial mouse, 75
serial ports, 61, 108
setting up computer, 142, 147-149
sharing software, 152
sheet feeds
    printers, 80
    scanners, 77
SIMMs (Single In-Line Memory Modules), 106, 159
slimline cases (system units), 62
slots, *see* expansion slots
software, 1-3, 159
    application software, 10
        backup programs, 151
        communications, 17, 92-93
        databases, 14-15, 25
        desktop publishing, 17, 154
        disk compression, 53
        educational applications, 17-18
        fax software, 92
        financial applications, 12-14, 24
        games, 18
        graphics applications, 15-16, 25, 156
        integrated applications, 17, 24, 156
        spreadsheet applications, 12-14, 24, 160
        utilities, 18, 160
        word processing, 10-12, 24, 160
    books, 104
    bundles, 21
    buying, 21-23, 119-120
    disk size, 28
    IBMs, 28
    Macintoshes, 28, 109

mouse drivers, 76
OCR (optical character recognition) software, 77
operating system software, 9-10, 158
PCs, 28
sharing, 152
system requirements, 26-28
sorting databases, 15
sound
   Macintoshes, 108-109
   sound cards, 95, 159
      buying, 99
      compatibility with CD-ROM drives, 100
      cost considerations, 99
spare parts, 142
speakers, 95, 99
spelling checkers, 11
spreadsheet programs, 12-14, 24, 160
standards
   buses, 46
   monitors, 67-68
   multimedia PCs, 97-98
stands (monitors), 70
starting computer system, 149
stores, 130-132, 134-138
storing papers, 5
subnotebook computers, 113, 160
SuperDrive (Macintosh floppy drives), 160
surge protectors, 103, 150
SVGA monitors, 67, 160
SX microprocessors, 44-45, 160
System operating system, 9, 39-40, 109, 160
system requirements for software, 26-28
system unit, 30, 160
   cases, 62-63
   expansion slots, 59-61
   floppy drives, 54-56
   hard drive, 52-54
   microprocessors, 31
   motherboard, 157
   power supply, 62
   processes, 31
   ventilation, 148
   see also hardware

T

tactility
   keyboard keys, 74
   mouse, 76
tape backup drives, 57

technical support, 142, 144
telephone lines, 93
Terminal communications program, 93
text holders for typing, 104
thesaurus, 11
toner (laser printers), 83
tower cases (system units), 62
track balls, 76, 160
transferring files, 87
transistors (microprocessors), 31-32, 43
TrueType fonts, 81-83
tuning monitors, 69-70
turning on/off computer system, 149-150
typing, *see* word processing

U-V

upgrades
   Macintoshes, 37
   memory
      Macintoshes, 106
      RAM, 48
   PCs, 37
user groups, 133
utility programs, 18, 160

ventilation (hardware), 148
VESA (Video Electronics Standards Association) buses, 46, 61, 69, 160
VGA monitors, 67, 160
video accelerator cards, 69
video adapter cards, 69
VRAM (video-RAM) (monitors), 107

W-Z

warranties, 141, 144-147
Windows, 9, 33, 38-39, 157
WinFax Pro fax software, 92
Word (Microsoft Corporation), 24
word processing
   applications, 10-12, 24, 160
   grammar checkers, 11
   spelling checkers, 11
   text holders, 104
   thesaurus, 11
WordPerfect (WordPerfect Corporation), 24
Works (Microsoft Corporation), 24
Wozniak, Steve, 32
wrist rests (keyboards), 74, 104